Peter Lupson is the author of a nu[mber of ... uni]versity French and German text b[ooks. For 12 ye]ars, he was Chief Examiner for GCE Advanced Level German for the University of Oxford, and he has also worked in educational publishing. He currently combines part-time English teaching and writing. In football, he has been a youth scout for a Premiership club in the north-west of England and he is honorary life president of a semi-professional club in North Wales. Peter is also the founder of a thriving church youth league on Merseyside.

THANK GOD FOR FOOTBALL!

Peter Lupson

First published in Great Britain in 2006

Society for Promoting Christian Knowledge
36 Causton Street
London SW1P 4ST

British Library Cataloguing-in-Publication Data
A catalogue record for this book is available from the British Library

ISBN 978–1–902694–30–6

5 7 9 10 8 6 4

Typeset by Graphicraft Ltd, Hong Kong
Printed in Great Britain by Ashford Colour Press

Produced on paper from sustainable forests

For my son, Mike, who set the ball rolling . . .

Also, for all members of Longcroft Football Club,
past and present.

Contents

Foreword

JOHN MOTSON

————◆•◆————

Week by week during the football season thousands upon thousands of fans converge on stadia across the country in the expectation of a thrilling afternoon's sport. The sight is so familiar that we just take it for granted. But to do so is a disservice to the memory of the very people who made it all possible – those enthusiasts of many years ago who had the vision, drive and energy to create the clubs that give so much enjoyment to so many. And their motives were not fame and fortune but the simple pleasure of friendship and the sheer fun of playing. Yet sadly most of the pioneers who planted the tiny seeds that have grown into our top clubs get little more than a passing mention in club histories.

It may come as a surprise to learn that nearly a third of the clubs that have played in the FA Premier League owe their existence to a church. It may be equally surprising to hear that very little is known about the founders of these famous clubs of church origin. In some cases even their names are wrong. This book sets the record straight. Drawing on original materials from a variety of sources, Peter Lupson has been able to bring these pioneers to life and to transport us back to the time in which they lived. Their remarkable contribution to our great national game is at last given the recognition it deserves. We have good reason to thank God for them.

Acknowledgements

This book has been assembled from hundreds of small items of information painstakingly gathered and sifted over a period of seven years. It would have been quite impossible for me to locate and collect each item individually and I am therefore indebted to the many people who have provided me with information that I would not otherwise have been able to access. Without their help the jigsaw would never have been complete.

My detailed research started at The Football Association headquarters where Geoff Thompson, the chairman, gave me his encouragement and support from the very beginning. Not only did he allow me access to The FA's resources but he also frequently discussed my progress with me. I am grateful, too, to David Barber, The FA archivist, for the help he gave me in locating materials and in scrutinizing my work.

I am grateful to Lord Mawhinney, chairman of The Football League, for his interest in, and support for this project. I very much appreciate the time he has given me.

Many thanks to John Motson for his contribution to this book and for his support, not least in allowing me the use of his magnificent library. Sorry I nearly wore out your photocopier, John!

I was able to make contact with almost all the official historians of the clubs featured in this book and I have had very productive telephone conversations or correspondence with them. I am particularly indebted to Arthur Bower of Barnsley, Gary James of Manchester City, Dave Juson of Southampton, Dick Mattick of Swindon Town and Andy Porter of Tottenham Hotspur who gave me hours of their time and who between them provided me with mountains of material. I hope you feel I have used it wisely.

Sadly, many of the churches that created the clubs in this book no longer exist although, thankfully, not all have gone. I have been privileged to meet the vicars of two of them, the Revd Allen Briscoe of St Peter's, Barnsley, and the Revd Simon Stevenette of Christ Church, Swindon. I thank them very much for their interest in this book. I am grateful, too, to the Revd Gavin Knight, vicar of St Andrew's, Fulham Fields, for putting me in touch with Morgan Phillips, the author of *Fulham We Love You.*

Without the resources of a great many libraries, archives and other centres it would have been impossible to write this book. I would like to express my gratitude for the invaluable help I have received from Matthew Andrews, the Bodleian Library, Oxford; Patrick Baird, Local Studies and History, Central Library, Birmingham; Steven Bashforth, Barnsley Central Library; Ken Beevers and Sharon Bolton, Bolton Archives and Local Studies; George Capel, Harrogate Library and Information Centre; Dr Rachel Cosgrave, Lambeth Palace Library, London; Edmund Dunne, Archives and Local Studies, Central Library, Manchester; Peter Ewart, Canterbury Cathedral Archives; Lynn Finn, Centre for Kentish Studies, Maidstone; Peter Forsaith, Methodist Studies Unit, The Wesley Centre, Oxford; Jeff Gerhardt, Bruce Castle Museum, Tottenham, London; Roger Hull, Liverpool Record Office; David Hollingworth, City Libraries, Southampton; Doreen Hopwood, Genealogist, Local Studies and History, Central Library, Birmingham; Angela Kenny, The Methodist Church Archives and History Committee, Harrow; Shirley McPherson, City of Westminster Archives Centre, London; Barry Mills, Bolton Archives and Local Studies; Daryl Moody, Swindon Local Studies Library; Tina Morton, Brent Archive, London; Margaret Parry, Liverpool Record Office; Dr John Pollard, Trinity Hall, Cambridge; Penny Rudkin, City Libraries, Southampton; Stuart Weir, Christians in Sport, Bicester; Madeleine Whitcombe, Cemeteries Dept, Dover District Council. I would also like to thank Alan Harding of Stratton, Swindon, for the information he gave me about Swindon Town's earliest matches and teams. I am embarrassed to admit that the names of the staff who helped me at the Flintshire County Reference Library, Mold, the Islington Local History Centre, London, and the London Metropolitan Archives have unfortunately slipped through the net. Please be assured of my gratitude for the assistance you so kindly gave me.

One of the pleasures in researching a book is meeting new people who are eager to help and who are generous with their time. I would like to thank Peggy Seymour, Jenny Simpson and Jack and Shirley Wiles, residents of the Queen's Park Estate in London, for the valuable information they gave me, a perfect stranger, about St Jude's Institute. The coffee and biscuits were also much appreciated!

Acknowledgements

Many thanks indeed to those of you who read my work at each stage and gave me such useful feedback. I greatly appreciate your perceptive comments and helpful observations and, not least, your encouragement at times when I was flagging. I must start with my wife, Evelyn, who despite being deprived of my company (and help in the garden!) during the long hours of writing, read each chapter carefully and cheerfully and never failed to give me her wholehearted support. My son, Mike, with his sharp eye for detail, ensured that inconsistencies in early drafts were quickly removed. I greatly appreciate his constructive criticism. My daughter, Karen, a history graduate, cast her historian's eye over some of the chapters and assured me that I was on the right lines. A huge relief, as I greatly value her opinion. My friends and colleagues at Kingsmead School, Hoylake, John Adamson and Dr Alan Roberts, read each chapter carefully and encouraged me enormously with their enthusiastic responses. Special thanks to Hugh Bradby, headmaster of Kingsmead, who despite his many responsibilities both inside and outside the school somehow found time to analyse my work and to comment on important details with his customary scholarly precision.

Passing reference has already been made to Morgan Phillips, author of *Fulham We Love You*, but he deserves much more. Morgan not only provided me with countless newspaper articles, club statistics and player profiles, copies of correspondence, extracts from booklets and brochures, photographs and much more besides, but he also inspired me with the breadth and depth of his scholarship and with his contagious enthusiasm for Fulham Football Club. Thank you, Morgan, for the many uplifting telephone conversations, for the voluminous correspondence, and above all, for your consistent encouragement. I'm now almost a Fulham supporter but loyalty to Norwich City forbids!

Finally, if I have omitted anyone whose name should have been included, please accept my sincere apologies. If you let me know, I will try to rectify this in any future printing.

Introduction

'I believe that all right-minded people have good reason to thank God for the great progress of this popular national game.' Those words were spoken by the legendary Lord Arthur Kinnaird, the holder of the still unbeaten record of nine FA Cup Final appearances and the longest serving chairman in the FA's history. Kinnaird, one of the leading Christian figures of the late Victorian era, would not have spoken those words lightly. As one of the pioneers at the fore-front of football's amazing development from an amateur sport played by a small number of well-to-do enthusiasts to the country's national game enjoyed by countless thousands, he was able to look back with gratitude on all that had been achieved and thank God for it.

Remarkably, of the 41 clubs that have played in the FA Premier League since its inception in the 1992–93 season, 12 also have good reason to take Lord Kinnaird's words to heart – they owe their very existence to churches. But these same clubs know very little about the circumstances that led to their birth or the people involved. This is hardly surprising in view of the fact that church teams, when they started, were the equivalent of today's public parks teams and did not keep extensive records of their activities. How could they possibly have guessed that one day they would become famous and that details about their founders, match results, players' records, minutes of early meetings, etc., would be of enormous interest to thousands of their future supporters? Furthermore, much of the limited source material that was once available has since been irretrievably lost through fire or neglect.

Despite these disadvantages, ground-breaking new information has been brought to light about the origins of these 12 clubs by approaching their history from a radically different angle. By drawing on contemporary newspaper accounts of local church activities and by accessing church sources such as parish magazines, personal correspondence, memoirs, career records, brochures and records of meetings, it has been possible to supplement – and sometimes to correct – information contained in club histories. How is it, then, that churches came to be involved in football?

In the latter half of the nineteenth century 'muscular Christianity' was born, a movement in which emphasis was placed on the practical expression of the Christian faith in service to others, as distinct from the development of personal piety. Muscular Christians brought about huge improvements in the living conditions and general quality of life of the poor and downtrodden, but it is not generally known that their contribution to society extended even beyond this – they also had a direct influence on the development of football.

Churches in general obviously welcomed the measures that led to improved living conditions and the consequent benefits to physical health, but many clergymen felt strongly that the physical welfare of the individual, though important, was not enough. A person's quality of life, they argued, depended as much on quality of character as on good health and a favourable environment. The moral and spiritual dimensions of the individual could not, therefore, be neglected. But was it possible, they wondered, to promote a person's – particularly a young person's – moral and spiritual health at the same time as their physical health? Was there an effective means of developing a healthy mind in a healthy body? They found their answer in the game of football as played in the famous public schools where the qualities of fair play, courage, self-control and unselfishness, as developed on the games field, were considered essential attributes of a Christian gentleman. It was the publication of Thomas Hughes' book *Tom Brown's Schooldays* in 1857 that had inspired the Christian sporting ethos of these schools.

Of course, there were many varieties of football in the public schools as, indeed, there were throughout England, and each version had its own set of rules. The best-known versions were those of top public schools such as Charterhouse, Eton, Harrow and Rugby but they were only played by the pupils or old boys of the respective school. Although kicking the ball was common to them all, the degree of kicking varied. At Charterhouse, for instance, a dribbling game was developed whereas at Rugby the emphasis was on catching and running. With so many different codes in existence, it was not possible for one school or club to play another.

Some attempt at establishing a unified code to enable different colleges to play each other was made at Cambridge University, first in 1846, then in 1848, and again in 1863. The breakthrough to uniformity at a national level came on 26 October 1863 when, at a meeting at Great Queen Street, London, 11 clubs in the London area formed themselves into an association called 'The Football Association' and agreed to play each other by a common set of rules. They named their version of the game 'Association football' after their group. In time, this form of football became known as 'soccer' from the letters 'soc' in the word 'Association' and spread throughout the world.

Whatever the version of football played at a particular public school, the influence of Thomas Hughes' book on the spirit of the game was unmistakable. And, in turn, many clergymen in the 1870s who were products of the public school system transmitted the values they had learned on the games field to the young people in their parishes. The result was a rapid spread of church cricket and football clubs throughout the country. In Birmingham alone, for instance, some 25 per cent of all football clubs formed between 1876 and 1884 were connected with religious establishments.

There was no uniform pattern in the formation of the many church football clubs that sprang up in the last quarter of the nineteenth century. While a clergyman was in some cases the actual founder, for example the Revd Tiverton Preedy of Barnsley FC and the Revd William Pitt of Swindon Town, the initiative also came from other sources. These were quite varied. For instance, members of the choir of Holy Trinity Church, Bordesley, started a cricket club that was to become Birmingham City FC; the headmaster of Christ Church Boys' School, Bolton, started a Sunday School football club that was to become Bolton Wanderers; and in the case of the church that gave birth to Manchester City, the initial nudge was given by the vicar's daughter. The story of each club is unique and makes fascinating reading but together they bring to life the remarkable period in which football began to capture the public imagination. It was an exciting time for football and this book introduces the reader to some of the exceptional people who made it so.

1

Aston Villa

———•◆•———

'The landmark church that gave birth to Aston Villa is to be demolished.' This announcement in the Birmingham *Evening Mail* on 20 July 2005 caused a stir not only in Birmingham, where the famous Aston Villa Football Club had been formed, but also in football circles far beyond the confines of the city itself. As one national newspaper reported, the building that faced demolition had not only produced one of the country's top clubs but was also associated with the birth of league football in England. Former England manager Sir Bobby Robson commented: 'We are very good in this country at taking down things like this. It's a shame when we uproot our treasured traditions. It's a memorial that is very precious.' Mark Bushell of the National Football Museum in Preston also voiced his concern that the building was to be destroyed: 'It will be a disaster if this is lost. Every football league in the world owes its existence to the one set up from this church.'

The imposing building in Lozells Road, the proposed destruction of which caused such widespread concern, was opened on 31 May 1865 as a Wesleyan Methodist church. It was originally known as the Aston Villa Wesleyan Chapel and it remained in Methodist hands until it was sold in 1962. As the name 'Aston Villa' became so closely associated with the renowned football club many people believed the chapel was named after it. In fact the reverse is true, as members of the chapel have frequently had to point out. 'Aston Villa' was originally the name of a large mansion that stood virtually opposite the chapel in the Aston district of Birmingham at the junction of Heathfield Road and Lozells Road. The building was a significant landmark and gave its name to the immediate locality, and it is from the Aston Villa locality that the chapel derives its name.

The club is born

The chapel attached great importance to its work with young people
and when two houses adjoining it were bought in 1871, the one closest was fitted out with classrooms to help cater for the over 300 young
people who attended the Sunday School. There they were grouped
according to age and gender and were given instruction in the essen-
tials of the Christian faith. One of the classes – the Young Men's Bible
Class – was the cradle of Aston Villa FC.

It was in 1872 that some of the members of the Young Men's Bible
Class decided to form a chapel cricket team and to play under the
name of 'The Aston Villa (Wesleyan) Cricket Club'. Of course, before
the name of the chapel could be used in this way, permission had
to be obtained first from the minister and probably also from the
circuit superintendent. (In Methodism local churches – known as
'Societies' – are grouped into circuits headed by a senior minister, the
superintendent.) However, in the case of Aston Villa chapel, the minister, 51-year-old Frederick Briggs, also conveniently happened to be
the circuit superintendent. Perhaps because, in the words of the 1892
Wesleyan Minutes of Conference, he was a man of 'gentleness, kindness and courtesy' who 'enjoyed the love and confidence of the people
in his charge', the cricketers had no difficulty in getting his consent.

It was obvious that the chapel was favourably disposed towards
sport because it featured prominently in another organization for
which it was responsible. This was a mission founded in 1878 in the
Lozells district by six young men who almost certainly attended
the same Bible class as the cricketers. The *Methodist Times* of 16 June
1910 reported that these six men 'who scorn the very idea of class distinction, and who recognize that spiritual and social work cannot be
divorced' started a work in a little mission hall in Porchester Street
that was to mushroom from 12 members in 1878 to nearly 1,200 in
1888. One of the founders of the mission, H. S. Yoxall, had come
across a large number of youths playing football on Sundays who
were 'rapidly developing into hooligans'. He befriended them and
persuaded them to attend a young men's Bible class at the mission on
Sundays. At first they only came if the weather was too bad for football but Yoxall promised he would get them a private field if they gave
up playing on Sundays. They agreed. All went well until Yoxall discovered that the old cowshed that he had fitted out as a dressing room

was being used for drinking. He decided, therefore, to join the team as a half-back and to keep an eye on them. He so impressed the youths with his skill on the pitch and by the way he treated them off it that they put a stop to their drinking, gave up playing on Sundays and became regular attenders at the Bible class.

Beginning with this little band of footballers, the mission went from strength to strength. Yoxall and his friends soon realized that, in addition to football, other activities could also be useful forms of outreach. They therefore started cycling, rambling and angling clubs and offered classes in arithmetic, writing, shorthand and music. To these were added a military band, an orchestral band and Saturday evening concerts. Eventually a gymnasium, games room, lounge, library and refreshment bar were provided. Such was the success of the mission that by 1898 it had developed into a Society (i.e. local church) in its own right, with its own minister, in purpose-built premises in Lozells Street.

The mission launched by the Aston Villa chapel was a spectacular success but the little cricket club started at the chapel in 1872 was destined for even greater things. Just two years after the club's formation a significant yet quite unexpected step was taken in its development. One Saturday afternoon in February 1874 four of its members, Jack Hughes, Frederick Matthews, Walter Price and William Scattergood, were invited to watch a football match between Moseley Grasshoppers and Handsworth Rugby Club on waste ground off Heathfield Road. At the time, football was still in its infancy in Birmingham, and played by only a handful of teams and they were keen to see what the game was like. They were immediately captivated by what they saw. When the match was over, they chatted under a gas lamp close to the chapel and took the decision to start up a football team, believing it was just the thing to keep the members of the cricket team fit during the long winter months. But they had to agree on which version of the game they would play as there were many varieties in England at the time. They felt that the particular game they had seen, which had been played under a crude set of Rugby rules, was too dangerous and they opted instead for what they considered the less harmful Association code. Association football (nicknamed 'soccer' from the letters 'soc' in the word 'Association') had been pioneered in London in 1863 and was beginning to spread across the country. They took the decision to call their new club 'The Aston Villa (Wesleyan) Football Club'.

Once again, as with the cricket club, permission had to be obtained to use the chapel's name. Frederick Briggs, who had supported the launch of the cricket club, was no longer in Birmingham having left to take up an appointment in Scarborough. The new minister, the Reverend Robert Balshaw, and the new circuit superintendent, the Reverend William Williams, would have to be approached. Fortunately Balshaw, a man known for his great humility and kindness, and Williams, a warm, approachable Welshman, were supportive.

Hughes, Matthews, Price and Scattergood immediately set about forming a committee. They appointed Billy Mason honorary secretary. His first task was to collect a one shilling (5p) fee from anyone wishing to become a playing member of the club. Fifteen members signed up. It was these 15 who provided almost all the players in the first Aston Villa teams.

The first matches

After practising together on some waste ground in Westminster Road, the young men were eager to contest their first match. But who could they play against? The few teams in Birmingham that were playing Association football were much too strong for them. One source states that a first tentative step was taken on a cold Saturday afternoon in January 1875 when Aston Park Unity provided the opposition. This match was played 14-a-side, under Sheffield rules, and ended when it became too dark to continue. Unity, who were leading 1–0, were declared winners.

However, most evidence suggests that Villa's historic first match was played much earlier, in March 1874, on a field lent for the occasion by a Mr Wilson. He had watched the players training in Westminster Road and was keen to help them. Surprisingly, the match was played 15-a-side against a rugby team from the neighbouring church of Aston Brook St Mary's. But why a rugby team? Simply because of the difficulty in finding football teams that were not too strong for the humble chapel side. To ensure as even a contest as possible, the first half was played under Rugby rules and the second half under Association football rules. Even different shaped balls were used in each half. Around 250 spectators saw Villa, captained by Walter Price, win the match 1–0. Jack Hughes was the scorer. The line-up was: William Scattergood (goalkeeper); W. Weiss,

Walter Price, F. Knight, Edward ('Teddy') Lee, Frederick Matthews, H. Matthews, Charles Midgley (defenders); and Jack Hughes, W. Such, H. Whateley, G. Page, A. H. Robbins, W. B. ('Billy') Mason and W. Sothers (forwards). (Some sources list G. Greaves and D. J. Stevens in the team in place of Knight and Sothers.)

Profiles of the founders

The names of Aston Villa's four founders are instantly recognizable in the line-up but remarkably, despite their importance in the club's history, there are no obituaries of them or other biographical records in either the Aston Villa FC archives or the Birmingham Central Library. It is almost as if they didn't exist. However, after much careful digging it has been possible to discover a few facts about Walter Price and William Scattergood.

Walter Price, Villa's first captain, who was 20 when he helped found the club, was born on 2 August 1854 at home at 28 Upper Tower Street, close to Birmingham's Jewellery Quarter. It is probably no coincidence, in view of the address, that his father was a jeweller. In 1881, at the age of 27, Walter was living at 5 Hylton Street (again, very close to the Jewellery Quarter) with his 57-year-old widowed mother, Mary, who worked in the jewellery industry, his younger sisters Eliza, 23, and Alice, 21, and his younger brother Edward, 20. The following year Walter married Annie Elkington, the daughter of an office clerk, at Birmingham Register Office. They had one child, a son Cornelius, named after Walter's father. Not surprisingly, perhaps, Walter followed his father and mother into the jewellery industry working as an electroplater and gilder, which involved engraving and coating jewellery. After a lifetime in the jewellery industry, Walter died of stomach cancer in Hallam Hospital, West Bromwich, on 23 August 1927 at the age of 73.

William Scattergood, his close friend, was born on 6 September 1855 at 30 St Vincent Street in the Ladywood district of Birmingham and was 19 when he co-founded the football club. His father was a pocketbook maker but later became a commercial clerk. William spent the whole of his working life employed in a brewery, first as a storekeeper, then as a drayman and eventually as a timekeeper. He never married. In 1901, at the age of 45, he was living at home at 3 Johnstone Street (not far from the Aston Villa chapel) with his

69-year-old widowed mother, Clara (a dressmaker), his two younger sisters, Florence, 34, and Nellie, 29, (both unmarried), and his five-year-old niece, Grace. William eventually moved further down the street to number 20 where he died of liver cancer on 14 March 1914 at the age of 58.

George Ramsay, the Scottish marvel

Although only two matches were played in the club's inaugural season, the players had clearly developed an appetite for football and in anticipation of more games in the 1875–76 season they decided to use Aston Park as their home base. According to Jack Hughes, Villa's first match there was in 1875 against Wednesbury Old Athletic, but unfortunately the date and result are not known. In all, some 15 matches were played that season, including memorable 5–1 victories over Grasshoppers and Heart of Oak and a 6–0 win against Walsall Albion.

The club was progressing well but its fortunes were to take a major upturn when a 20-year-old Scotsman who had left Scotland to take up a job as a clerk with a firm of brassfounders in Birmingham, came across the Villa players in a practice match one Saturday afternoon in the autumn of 1876. George Ramsay was an outstanding footballer and because he found the pull of the game irresistible, he had deliberately set off for Aston Park in the hope of finding a match. When he saw the Villa practice match he asked if he could join in. The players readily agreed. But it was soon obvious to them that the newcomer was no ordinary footballer. Ramsay was a master of the art of dribbling and his skill mesmerized the Villa enthusiasts, whose own play he later described as nothing more than 'a dash at the man and a big kick at the ball'. When the game was over, the Scottish marvel was immediately invited to play for the club in the forthcoming match against Stafford Road. He was only too pleased to accept. In fact, he played on several more occasions that season and such was the respect he commanded that he was made captain in time for the start of the next season.

Ramsay had a profound influence on the club. He attracted better players, reorganized training techniques, and introduced the passing style of football he had learned in Scotland. Villa's performances improved dramatically. As a player, Ramsay delighted spectators with his dazzling display of ball control but his polo cap and long white trousers must also have provided something of a spectacle. Unfortunately his playing days came to an abrupt end in 1880, after an injury in a match against Nottingham Forest from which he never fully recovered. However, his heart remained with the club and he continued to serve it for the rest of his life. He was a committee member from 1880 to 1886, secretary from 1886 to 1926 and finally a vice-president until his death in October 1935.

Even though Villa had begun to play better football under his leadership, Ramsay realized that the club could not make real progress unless it had a home of its own where it could charge admission. The problem was solved when he was out for a stroll with fellow committee member John Lindsay one Sunday afternoon in 1876. They came across a grazing field just off the Wellington Road in the nearby village of Perry Barr. Ramsay felt it would make a suitable pitch. The field was duly acquired, the pitch was roped off, and the first match was played there on 30 September 1876 against Wednesbury Town.

Villa's first presidents

Although Ramsay had become the undisputed leader of the club, mention should also be made of the two men who were its earliest figureheads, Henry Haynes Hartshorne and the Reverend Charles Beecroft, respectively Villa's first and second presidents.

Henry Hartshorne ran two Bible classes at the Aston Villa chapel, one for adults and another for young men. It was in the latter class that he taught the founders of Aston Villa Football Club. These young men held Hartshorne in very high regard and when they formed the club in 1874 they invited him to become their president. The son of an ironmonger, Hartshorne was born in 1833 in Old Swinford, near Stourbridge. He spent the whole of his working life in the drapery business, mostly as a commercial traveller, and was in this employment right up until his death at the age of 80 in Birmingham in 1913. He seems to have enjoyed a fairly comfortable income because he could afford the services of a governess and servant at the family home in St Peter's Road (near the chapel), where he lived with his wife, Hannah, their six children, his brother-in-law and two nieces at the time the club was founded.

Hartshorne was Villa president until 1877 when he was succeeded by Charles Beecroft, a Methodist minister serving in the Wellington circuit in Shropshire some 40 miles away. Beecroft was president for only one year. A butcher's son, he was born in 1845 in Lowestoft, Suffolk. He was ordained a Methodist minister in 1870 and after appointments in Yorkshire and Cheshire, he came to Wellington in 1876 for a three-year term. From Wellington he went to Chorley in Lancashire and, after serving in two further circuits, emigrated to New Zealand in 1888, where he remained for the rest of his life. It is a measure of the respect in which he was held there that in 1908 he attained the country's top position in Methodism – president of the New Zealand Conference. He died in Onehunga in 1913 at the age of 68.

William McGregor joins the club

The same year that Beecroft became president of Aston Villa FC, a 31-year-old Scotsman who was to change the whole course of football history became a member of the committee. William McGregor had left his native Perthshire in 1870 to take advantage of the business opportunities that Birmingham presented. He bought a linen draper's shop on the corner of Brearley Street and Summer Lane (in Aston) where he was to remain in business for the rest of his life. McGregor had got to know fellow Scot George Ramsay and the two men had become firm friends. Ramsay managed to persuade McGregor to become involved with Aston Villa. It proved to be an astute move because McGregor was a visionary and energetic leader and he helped make Villa the most successful and prestigious club in the country. Even today there is a visible reminder of his influence: it was at his suggestion that the Scottish national symbol of a lion rampant was adopted as the club's badge. But his name in football will forever be associated with something even greater than the famous club itself. He was the creator of the Football League.

McGregor was a committed Christian widely respected for his honesty and integrity. The Reverend W. G. Percival, a pastor at the Congregational church in Wheeler Street, Aston, where McGregor worshipped for over 40 years, said at his funeral service that the best thing about him 'was not so much the genial, kindly, honest sportsman, but it was the Christian behind it all'. He described him as 'a man of absolutely unblemished personal character'. Charles Crump, president of the Birmingham County Football Association, stated in the local press that he 'stood for all that was best and cleanest in the great game of football'. People found it impossible to dislike him even if they disagreed with him, and it was said of him that he never made an enemy and never lost a friend.

It did not take long for McGregor to make his presence felt at Aston Villa. One particular problem that faced the committee was the players' drinking habits. Many of them were regularly giving training a miss, preferring to spend their time in local pubs, and some even turned up drunk for matches. Something had to be done. Determined to instil new habits in the players, McGregor, a lifelong teetotaller, decided to rent a room at a coffee house in Aston High Street and to compel them to attend social gatherings and musical events each Monday during the season. It might be more than just a coincidence that Villa enjoyed considerable success not long afterwards.

McGregor and Ramsay were a formidable partnership. Within three years of McGregor's arrival they had established the club as a force to be reckoned with in local football. A 21–0 win against Small Heath Swifts gives some indication of their strength at the time. The recruitment in 1878 of 19-year-old Archie Hunter, another Scot who had come to Birmingham in search of work, was a particularly inspired move. Hunter, whose impressive playing style and sense of sportsmanship made him a favourite with the fans, was considered to be the best centre-forward of his day and he was one of football's first superstars. His influence in the side was considerable and when Ramsay retired from playing in 1880 through injury, Hunter took over the captaincy.

Of course, the only games they played during this period were either friendlies or local cup ties. No league of any kind existed. The first major trophy was won in 1880, when, under the captaincy of George Ramsay, Villa beat Saltley College 3–2 in the final of the Birmingham Senior Cup. There were only two survivors of the first recorded team of 1874 in the side, Billy Mason and Teddy Lee, although Jack Hughes also took part as an umpire (assistant referee).

The following season Villa enjoyed even more success, winning 21 of their 25 games, gaining their second trophy, the Staffordshire Cup, and reaching the fourth round of the FA Cup. In the 1882–83 season they reached the quarter-finals of the FA Cup for the first time, and a year later, in a series of prestigious friendlies, they took on and defeated some of the most famous teams in the land. They were now a force to be reckoned with beyond the confines of Birmingham. By 1885 the club clearly felt it had come of age. Professionalism was legalized that year and Villa took the opportunity to abandon their amateur status.

The FA Cup is won

Having turned professional in 1885, Villa's first real taste of glory came two years later when they won the FA Cup and were propelled among the game's élite. After beating Glasgow Rangers in the semi-final (it was the last time Scottish teams entered the competition), they met Midlands rivals West Bromwich Albion in the final. When the result was known – a 2–0 win for Villa – thousands of jubilant supporters went wild with delight in the streets of Birmingham. Their celebrations continued long into the night, culminating in a rapturous welcome for the team at New Street station at 3 a.m. on Sunday morning. The *Birmingham Daily Post* now proudly proclaimed them the 'champion team of the United Kingdom'. But this cup success was to have even greater significance. It gave William McGregor the platform he needed to spearhead a reform that would solve the most pressing problem in football as he saw it. As a representative of one of the most successful clubs in the country, he now had the authority and credibility to proceed.

McGregor forms the Football League

What was the problem that McGregor found so intolerable? The answer can be summed up in a single word – friendlies. These were the staple football diet of the day, and it was apparent that spectators had lost their appetite for them. The reasons were many: they lacked the excitement and competitive edge of cup ties, they were often so one-sided that they were not worth watching, and kick-off times and the duration of games were frequently altered on the day without notice. Sometimes teams turned up short of players and had to enlist the services of spectators. Furthermore, games were often cancelled with a minimum of notice or none at all, and it was not unusual for a team to fail to turn up for a game because they had found more attractive opposition elsewhere. The result of this chaotic situation was an alarming dip in attendances. For professional clubs such as Aston Villa, who had a wage bill to meet, the situation was disastrous.

The impetus for change came one winter's evening in 1886 when McGregor was chatting with his close friend Joe Tillotson in the latter's coffee house at 91 Alma Street. In the course of their conversation, mention was made of the forthcoming friendly between Aston Villa and Walsall Town. As Walsall were no match for Villa, and the outcome was inevitable, Tillotson predicted that the attendance would be poor. By now Villa so dominated Midlands football that their supporters had become tired of a succession of uneven contests against inferior local sides. As a result they stayed away in large numbers. Clearly, something had to be done, but what? McGregor and Tillotson discussed the matter at some length. Although the precise details of their discussion are not known, one thing is certain – the idea for a football league emerged from it.

McGregor left Tillotson's coffee house that evening in no doubt that he had hit on the solution to the problem of what he called the 'lax and loose system' of casual friendlies and occasional cup matches: 'What was wanted was a fixity of fixtures.' Surely the prospect of exciting, guaranteed fixtures played on a regular basis between a designated number of top clubs, with points awarded according to results, would get spectators back to the grounds they had deserted?

The first step was to win the support of other clubs. After a constructive and encouraging preliminary meeting with the representatives of seven clubs at Anderton's Hotel in Fleet Street, London, on 23 March 1888 to discuss the idea, McGregor called a further meeting at the Royal Hotel, Manchester, on 17 April to consider the formation of a league of 12 clubs, to elect officers and draw up rules. (He had set a limit of 12 simply because this was the maximum number that would fit into the available Saturday afternoon slots in a season.) The delegates responded enthusiastically and the Football League was born. The 12 clubs who became founder members were Accrington, Aston Villa, Blackburn Rovers, Bolton Wanderers, Burnley, Derby County, Everton, Notts County, Preston North End, Stoke, West Bromwich Albion and Wolverhampton Wanderers. McGregor was elected chairman and was made the first president. On 23 July the fixture list for the new season was drawn up and on Saturday 8 September 1888, in perfect weather, the first ever Football League matches kicked off.

Under McGregor's inspired leadership the Football League went from strength to strength. When he retired from the presidency in 1893, only five years after the League had been founded, he could look back with satisfaction over its growth from 12 clubs to 31, and from one division to two. His qualities as an administrator were clearly defined in his obituary in the *Birmingham Gazette* of 21 December 1911: 'it may be said that he has had no superior, if an equal, in the council chambers of the game. He possessed a statesmanlike mind, and everything he suggested was prompted simply and solely by his desire to further the best interests of the sport he loved so well, and was marked by sound common sense and judgment.' At a memorial ceremony in his honour in 1912 he was described as 'a thoughtful, tactful and wise counsellor and legislator, full of the highest ideals for the game to be played and controlled in clean, honest and manly fashion. He has left a record and influence on the game that will make his memory honoured and revered.'

Momentous developments

Of course, the whole time McGregor was involved in his history-making developments with the Football League he did not cease to be active in the affairs of Aston Villa. It is easy to forget, in view of his achievements on the national stage, that he was also a guiding hand at Villa during the most significant period in the club's history – from 1894 to 1900. There were momentous developments, both on and off the pitch, in the course of these few years. On the playing side Villa enjoyed success of a kind that very few clubs have equalled since: they won the League championship five times (1894, 1896, 1897, 1899, 1900) and the FA Cup twice (1895, 1897), the most memorable season being 1896–97 when the coveted League and Cup double was won.

There were also important milestones off the pitch. Recognizing that the club needed to be organized more properly along business lines, McGregor proposed in 1889 that it should become a limited company. It was committee member Fred Rinder, however, who led the long hard-fought campaign that eventually brought about a change of status on 20 January 1896 when the first board meeting of The Aston Villa Football Club (Limited) was held. The following year Villa moved from the inadequate Perry Barr ground to their new ground, Villa Park, still the club's home today.

The death of McGregor

In 1908 McGregor's wife, Jessie, died. It was a blow from which he never fully recovered and from that time his own health began to deteriorate. By 1910 it had declined to such an extent that he had to have major surgery, which left him considerably weakened. The following year, a few days after receiving a gold medal on 4 December in recognition of 20 years' service to the Football Association, he contracted a chill which brought on a very severe attack of gastritis. His condition became critical and it was decided that an operation was his only chance of survival. It appeared to have been successful but heart problems quickly developed and on Wednesday 20 December 1911, McGregor died. He was 65. There can be little doubt that, had he taken the advice he had been given to rest, his health would not have deteriorated so rapidly in his last year, but he was unable to resist the temptation to take an active part in football affairs.

His funeral took place on Saturday 23 December at the Wheeler Street Congregational Chapel where he had worshipped. His body had been taken to his home at 8 Salisbury Road and from there an imposing procession, which included representatives of the sporting world from all parts of the country, made its way to Wheeler Street. Respectful crowds lined the streets to pay their tribute. Following the service, McGregor was buried in the picturesque graveyard of the parish church of St Mary's, Handsworth.

McGregor's obituary in the *Birmingham Gazette* of 21 December gives a clear indication of the high esteem in which he was held:

Mr McGregor was a personality in Birmingham. He was beloved by all who knew him. Our old friend was an astute judge of character and was a born leader of men; simple in his tastes, conscientious in his business capacity, a man of the highest integrity, and one who never sought publicity or notoriety. We do not believe he ever made an enemy; he certainly never lost a friend; and the sporting world in general is the poorer by his death.

There were a number of memorials to McGregor. First, a cheque in his memory was donated to the Titanic Disaster Fund in 1912. This ill-fated ship had sunk on 15 April 1912 after hitting an iceberg in the Atlantic on its maiden voyage from Southampton to New York. In June 1912 a second cheque was presented in his memory, this time by the Football League on behalf of its 40 member clubs to endow a bed in his name in Birmingham General Hospital. A portrait of him was hung near to the bed. On 25 October 1913 a drinking fountain on the corner of Lozells Road at Six Ways, Aston, was unveiled in McGregor's memory. The crowd attending the ceremony was so great that the police had to stop the traffic. The fountain was later relocated to Villa Park where it was placed, appropriately enough, in the restaurant named after McGregor in the Trinity Road Stand. Sadly, it went missing after the stand was redeveloped in recent years.

Though he never sought publicity or notoriety, McGregor's name has not been forgotten in Birmingham and it lives on in McGregor Close off Station Road, appropriately almost within the very shadow of the Villa Park stadium.

The club/chapel link

It is not known how much involvement Aston Villa FC had with the Aston Villa chapel during the momentous years when the club was growing in status and fame and when McGregor founded the Football League. Although at some point the word 'Wesleyan' was dropped from its title, the name 'Aston Villa' continued in use, suggesting that there was no formal break with the chapel until 1896 when the club became a limited company. However, it seems that even after 1896 the relationship between club and chapel remained friendly. When a service was held at the chapel in May 1935 to commemorate the seventieth anniversary of its opening, the chairman of Aston Villa FC, Jack Jones, the club secretary, William Smith, and several players all attended. But such bonds as may have existed were finally severed in 1962 when Methodist worship at the chapel ceased and the building was sold. And with the announcement in 2005 that the building was to be demolished came the sad realization that even the visible link with the club's origin was about to disappear. No wonder there was a public outcry.

2

Barnsley

———•◦•———

The year 1912 will forever be etched in the consciousness of supporters of Barnsley Football Club – it was the year in which the club tasted national glory by winning the FA Cup for the first and only time in its history. The match ball from that momentous Cup Final victory over West Bromwich Albion is now one of the club's most treasured possessions, but, surprisingly, its first home was not in Barnsley at all but in Islington, London, where it was proudly displayed in the study of a Church of England clergyman until his death in 1928. But how did a London clergyman come to own this symbol of the club's greatest triumph? Simply because in the euphoria of victory, the club remembered the man to whom it owed its very existence. By presenting the Cup Final ball to the Reverend Tiverton Preedy immediately after the match, Barnsley Football Club was honouring its founder.

Tiverton Preedy, founder of the club

Tiverton Preedy was born on 22 January 1863 in the small seaside resort of Hunstanton in Norfolk to Charles Preedy, an estate agent, and his wife Mary. Tiverton was the second of their four children, three boys and a girl. He attended Bloxham School near Sleaford in Lincolnshire. Later he felt a calling to the service of the poor and deprived, and so, in 1885 at the age of 22, he entered Lincoln Theological College to train for the Anglican ministry. Significantly, the founder of the college, Edward Benson, had been an assistant master at Rugby School from 1852 to 1858, the school made famous for its sporting values by Thomas Hughes in his book *Tom Brown's Schooldays*. The book was published when Benson was working there and he was almost certainly influenced by the sports ethos that prevailed in the school. Benson became firmly convinced that sport, with its emphasis on manliness and fair play, could be a force for moral good in the education of young people. He incorporated this belief into the training of the students at the theological college he founded in Lincoln in 1874. It was here that Tiverton Preedy caught the vision of sport as a moral agent and he embraced this 'muscular Christian' notion with great enthusiasm. Little did he know what significance this would have for the Yorkshire mining town of Barnsley.

Preedy arrives at St Peter's, Barnsley

Preedy was ordained deacon in 1887 (the year of Queen Victoria's Golden Jubilee), and priest the following year. Obeying his calling to the poor and deprived, he took up an appointment in 1887 as Assistant Stipendiary Curate at St Peter's Church in a squalid part of central Barnsley. In common with other industrial towns of the Victorian period, Barnsley was largely populated by manual workers who lived with their families in insanitary, cramped conditions in districts where terraced houses had been hastily erected without regard to comfort or hygiene. In such districts poverty and disease were rife, and for countless numbers of miners the principal means of escape from the miseries of life was alcohol, which was easily and cheaply available in the many public houses that had sprung up in working-class localities. But with alcohol came widespread drunkenness and drink-related violence, as well as many pitiful cases of child neglect by inebriated parents. This was the environment in which St Peter's started life in 1872.

St Peter's had been set up as a mission under the umbrella of St Mary's, the parish church of Barnsley, to help relieve the suffering that was so prevalent in the area. The man appointed to run the mission was the Reverend John Lloyd Brereton. By 1887 Brereton's work had grown to such proportions that St Peter's was officially licensed as a new parish district and funds were raised to build a new church. Clearly, Brereton alone could not cope with the demands of the district, and so it was that Tiverton Preedy was appointed to assist him. Preedy embraced the challenge wholeheartedly.

The birth of Barnsley St Peter's Football Club

During his settling-in period in Barnsley, Preedy felt it would be a good idea to find a sports club where he could make contact with Barnsley people and pursue his sporting interests. He soon joined Barnsley Rugby Club. However, he did not remain a member for long, feeling compelled to leave on a matter of principle. As he explained many years later in 1926 in an interview with the *Church Times*, he had resigned 'in protest'. The reason for this was because the club, which normally played its games on Saturdays, had arranged a match for Good Friday. Preedy refused to play sport on the day that Christ was crucified and he immediately walked out.

His action that day was to have huge significance for football in Barnsley. As he was walking down the street away from the club, he chanced upon some young men outside a public house and overheard them discussing the formation of a soccer team. Preedy was captivated by the idea and joined in their conversation. As the discussion developed, his vision and infectious enthusiasm made a great impression on the young men and they quickly realized that here was the man to lead them. Once more, Preedy leapt to the challenge. The prophetic words he spoke to them that day give some indication of his determination and sense of purpose: 'We will start an Association club such as the Rugbyites will not crush out.'

The Rugbyites in Barnsley held football in very low regard at the time. It was considered the poor man's sport, and enjoyed no social prestige. Rugby, on the other hand, attracted the affluent and influential members of the town, and they played their games in a pleasant area far removed from the slums of St Peter's. In forming a football team Preedy knew that he would not enjoy the support of members of the social class to which he belonged. But, more importantly, he realized that football could provide him with a vehicle for reaching out to the working-class community of St Peter's. It would give him a common interest with the young men of the district and a language that they could understand – the language of sport. It was not to be the only time in Preedy's long ministry that he would use sport as a means of outreach to the community that he served.

Preedy was a born leader and a gifted organizer, and it was natural that his drive and energy would quickly turn talk into action. He immediately set about forming the club that the young men wanted.

His first step was to choose a name that would signal the commitment of the church to the community. That name was Barnsley St Peter's Football Club. It was appropriate, therefore, that at the club's inaugural meeting on Tuesday 6 September 1887 the two clergymen of St Peter's should be elected as officers of the club. Preedy became financial secretary while the vicar, the Reverend Brereton, was made president.

The club's first president

Coincidentally, Brereton, like Preedy, originated from Norfolk. He was born in 1843 in Brinton, a small village between Fakenham and the seaside resort of Cromer. He was educated at St Edmund Hall in the University of Oxford, and after graduation in 1866 he trained to become a clergyman of the Church of England. Again, like Preedy, his first post was in Barnsley; he became curate of St Mary's in 1867, staying until 1881 when he moved to St Peter's.

The early days of the new St Peter's Football Club were hard. Preedy later recalled that 'Rugger was the game up to then and the new style met with strenuous opposition. The Press, the people, everyone seemed to be against us. But we fought on.' This opposition was gradually overcome by the fact that St Peter's Church identified itself unreservedly with the club. As the Anglican Church was a strong symbol of social respectability, the attachment of the name of St Peter's to the football club gave it increasing credibility and respect.

'Preedy's Team'

Preedy's involvement with Barnsley St Peter's FC was considerable. Although officially financial secretary, he was active in every aspect of the club's life. Apart from raising money, he was a player, he recruited players, he arranged fixtures, he secured match officials for fixtures, and he mediated in disputes. Through his personal enthusiasm and energy he laid the secure foundations on which membership of the Football League and success in the FA Cup were eventually achieved. It is no wonder then that the team became known locally as 'Preedy's Team'.

On Saturday 17 September 1887, 11 days after the club had been officially formed, Barnsley St Peter's played their first match. It was a friendly, away to Manor House. St Peter's turned out in maroon and navy blue striped jerseys, the colours they sported in their first two seasons. 'The Saints', as they were initially known (after 'St Peter's'), won 4–1. Preedy played as a forward. (He was to feature in four more games that season, scoring once, but he did not play in subsequent seasons.) Lacking changing facilities in the small building that initially served as St Peter's Church, the players were offered a room in the Dove Inn directly across the road. This also served for the club's early committee meetings. It would seem highly unlikely that any alcohol was consumed there as Preedy was a staunch advocate of the Temperance Movement.

The St Peter's club prospered and quickly attracted new recruits. After only a few weeks there were sufficient players to form a second team. However, there was a rapid turnover of players in each of the first three seasons and the lack of continuity meant that the standard of play was never high enough to enable the club to play in any kind of league. Games during this period were, therefore, mostly friendlies with occasional local cup matches.

The St Peter's players of the early years were amateurs in the strictest sense of the word. They paid membership subscriptions, they received no expenses, and they even bought their own kit. They played purely for the love of the game. However, there was no strict sense of loyalty to any one club in those days. Players simply wanted to play, and if their own club had no match they would look for a game elsewhere. Only professionals were restricted to one club. Because of the frequent comings and goings of players, not one of those who played in that first match was still in the St Peter's team when regular league football arrived in the 1890–91 season.

Nevertheless, although a settled team did not emerge during the first three seasons, the standard of play had improved sufficiently for the club to be admitted to the Sheffield and District League in 1890. Of course, the arrival of league football meant that higher standards of play had to be maintained, something that would only be possible if a fixed squad could be recruited. With the comings and goings of the amateur players, stability could only be achieved by recruiting professionals. Ever the realist, Tiverton Preedy quickly recognized this and he did not shy from taking the step towards professionalism.

The nature of the early matches

What kind of football would spectators have seen St Peter's play in those early years? Preedy's reminiscences are revealing:

> I remember playing honest, robust and straightforward football when the sporting press were not frightened of seeing honest, good, sound shoulder charging. Those were the days when we had a good charge and a knock head over heels. Those were the days when referees did not blow the whistle so often, and those were the days when football was real football and shoulder charging was real charging without any nasty tricks of the trade.

Although Preedy clearly enjoyed the rough and tumble of football as it was played at the time, he expected high standards of sporting behaviour from players and spectators alike. Such was his disgust at the behaviour of supporters of fierce local rivals Ardsley Old that he would not allow a match between them and St Peter's to go ahead during the 1888–89 season. In a letter to the local press he stated his reasons:

> I regret I am unable to advise my committee to consent to the match being played on the Ardsley ground, but I cannot satisfy myself that, judging from past experience, the conduct and language of a large portion of spectators would be such if the match was played there . . . as to be conducive of either a pleasant or a well-played game.
>
> We cannot too strongly bear in mind that if we allow the football field to degenerate simply into a resort for people who will not conduct themselves aright, we shall lose the support of those people who encourage football for the game's sake, and who are its only true supporters.
>
> I am quite certain too that unless the committee of such clubs as Ardsley and St Peter's – leading clubs in the district – use every endeavour to put down the disagreeable and offensive language too frequently heard on football fields, respectable people will have no alternative but to stay away altogether.

The move to Oakwell

In addition to founding the club and raising its profile, Preedy was also responsible for finding it a permanent home. From the steps of St Peter's he could see open fields across the valley in an area known as Oakwell. These were owned by Arthur and Guy Senior, who were also the owners of Barnsley Brewery which stood next to them. Preedy immediately saw that the area would provide an ideal location for a football pitch and he applied to the brothers for the hire of one of the fields. His request was turned down. Preedy made repeated applications, but without success. Never one to be deterred, he put his case convincingly to Arthur's wife, and she eventually persuaded her husband to rent him the field. There was one important condition, however. It was made very clear to Preedy that 'You can have the field so long as you behave yourselves!' Although there is some dispute as to whether the club's original ground is the present Oakwell enclosure or the field that adjoined it, there is no doubt that Barnsley would not be playing at Oakwell today had it not been for Preedy's persistence.

Securing a ground was an important step, but Preedy could see that St Peter's could only make real progress as a club if its finances were on a firm footing. To ensure that there was a steady income, he introduced an admission charge of threepence to the field at Oakwell. This provided a valuable source of revenue to help finance the payments made to the club's professional players.

The club's first trophy

Preedy was passionate about the club he had founded, but his involvement with football in Barnsley extended beyond St Peter's. One development in particular shows that he had much broader vision. In 1890 local rugby clubs had introduced a new cup competition. However, the manner in which funds had been raised for it aroused the suspicion of the town's football community. Furthermore, the false claim had been made in the local press that St Peter's would be taking part. This untrue statement infuriated Preedy and prompted him to set about persuading leaders of local football clubs that it was time to introduce a cup competition of their own. The result was the birth of the Barnsley Charity Association Football Union on 19 March 1891 at the King's Head Hotel, where it was agreed that a silver cup should be purchased costing £75 and weighing 140 ounces. Preedy was elected the Union's first secretary.

The final of the first Barnsley Charity Cup took place on 19 March 1892 at Shaw Lane Cricket Ground, Barnsley. St Peter's and the unfancied Ecclesfield were the finalists. They were watched by a crowd of about 6,000 – the largest ever for a football match in Barnsley. So confident were St Peter's of winning that they had hired a band to lead their victorious team to the cup headquarters at the King's Head, playing 'See the Conquering Hero Comes'. However, this presumption was misplaced as, against all the odds, Ecclesfield shocked the local football world with a 3–2 win. Preedy, with an eye to the future, immediately signed six of the Ecclesfield team. His judgement proved to be astute. St Peter's won the trophy for the next two seasons.

Preedy leaves Barnsley

The year 1893 marked the beginning of a new era in the history of St Peter's. The Charity Cup victory brought the club its first trophy, and won for it a large following in the town. In the wake of this triumph more success was to follow. But 1893 was significant for another reason: it was the year that the driving force behind the club, Tiverton Preedy, left Barnsley and set off for London to take up a curacy at St Clement's Church in City Road, Islington.

Preedy had been held in very high esteem in Barnsley. His contribution to the sporting life of the town, though significant, was not the major part of his involvement with the people of Barnsley. He was much more concerned with their spiritual welfare. This was recognized at a special gathering at the King's Head Hotel attended by the mayor and other civic dignitaries one Saturday evening in late April. The occasion was reported in the *Barnsley Chronicle* of 22 April 1893 and it is illuminating to read some of the tributes that were paid to Preedy. The mayor, Dr Halton, while

> differing widely as he did from Mr Preedy in religious belief . . . could yet honestly say that he has esteemed the work Mr Preedy had done in Barnsley, both religiously and socially. He believed Mr Preedy had done an immense amount of good work in that part of the town where his mission had been, and he knew he had done it in a Christian-like manner, and had undoubtedly elevated the working class and given them higher aims to work for. He had shown them there was something more in this world than the actual getting [of] food and drink for the sustaining of our bodies.

Another speaker, Councillor Raley, told the audience: 'Mr Preedy had been . . . a fearless pastor – if there was any work wanted doing, or any place wanted visiting, no matter what the dangers were, you would always find him there.' C. J. Tyas, the chairman of Preedy's testimonial committee, highlighted one of Preedy's defining qualities: 'A predominant trait in Mr Preedy's character while he had been in Barnsley was the extraordinary conscientiousness he had displayed in all his duties, whether religious or secular.'

Preedy had also established a reputation as a preacher while in Barnsley, a fact pointed out by the *Islington Gazette* of 27 April 1928 in its review of his life: 'At Barnsley his direct and forceful mission preaching made a great impression on the mining population of the district, and his name became well known throughout Yorkshire.'

The evening concluded with the presentation of a £60 testimonial to Preedy, a generous amount in those days. In addition to the testimonial, he received a walking stick, a pipe and a tobacco pouch from the players of St Peter's FC.

The change of name to Barnsley Football Club

Once Preedy had left Barnsley, the link with St Peter's Church was effectively broken. Only the club's president had any connection with the church, but his influence was negligible. Consequently, in the summer of 1895, two years after Preedy had left, a campaign was started by a Mr E. Jaeger and his 'small army' to remove the name 'St Peter's' from the club's title, and to rename the club 'Barnsley Town Association Football Club'. Jaeger also pointed out that if the link with St Peter's were formally severed by removal of the church's name, matches could be played on Good Fridays. The club's ruling committee was sympathetic to Jaeger's proposals, but preferred the name 'Barnsley Association Football Club'. In spite of a majority of votes in favour of this proposal, the name change could not go ahead on a point of order – it had not been placed on the agenda. Two more years of debate and disagreement ensued before a new name was finally agreed and adopted. That name was 'Barnsley Football Club', and the club played under this new name for the first time at the start of the 1897–98 season. It is remarkable that it took four years from Preedy's departure for 'St Peter's' to be dropped from the club's title. Preedy had so firmly established the club's identity as an integral part of the church that a change of name could not be undertaken lightly.

Preedy's work in Islington

When Preedy left for London it was in the full knowledge that he was embarking on a ministry that would stretch him to his limits. Islington suffered even greater poverty and deprivation than the St Peter's district of Barnsley, and he knew that the pastoral demands on him would be huge. C. J. Tyas was quick to point this out when, at Preedy's testimonial gathering, he told everyone that 'Mr Preedy was leaving them . . . for a new sphere of labour in London – a district where he would require all the strength and the energy they knew him to possess.' But Preedy's passionate love for the people he served, together with his indomitable faith in God, were the mainsprings from which he drew the strength and inspiration to meet the enormous challenge that confronted him.

And he more than met it. For 35 years he served his parishioners in Islington in their deprivation and misery with absolute devotion, bringing 'Sunshine in the Slums' as one newspaper put it. So greatly was he loved and revered there that when he died in 1928 thousands were present at his burial at Islington Cemetery. But in all the time he lived in London he never forgot Barnsley nor Barnsley Football Club. As will be seen, the links with that town and club were not to be broken.

Preedy served four years as curate at St Clement's, before becoming priest-in-charge of All Saints Mission in Islington in 1897. The mission had been newly founded in White Lion Street – according to *The Sportsman* 'one of the most unlovely spots in London' – by members of the wealthy West End congregation of All Saints' Church in Margaret Street. When Preedy arrived there the buildings were dilapidated, being nothing more than the cowsheds of a local dairyman. The little house in which he lived had no furniture. Having no bed, he slept on the floor using his coat for a blanket.

Preedy's neighbours in the dismal streets of the district mostly earned their living as costermongers (fruit sellers) or flower sellers. Once again, it was through sport that Preedy reached out to those around him, not this time through football, because the slums of London had too little open space in which to play, but through boxing and wrestling. He set up a full-sized boxing ring and two billiard tables in the crypt of his mission hall. Here he founded the Ashdown Athletic Club, which was to become famous in sporting circles for the boxers and wrestlers it produced. Terry Allen, who was to become the world flyweight boxing champion, came here as a boy, while 8 of the 12 wrestlers who represented Great Britain in the Paris Olympics of 1924 were members of Preedy's club. One of Ashdown's greatest wrestlers was George Mackenzie. He represented Great Britain in five Olympic Games from 1908 and officiated at four more. In November 1956 he was chosen to carry the Union Jack in the parade of Olympic teams at Melbourne. It was a fitting climax to a great sporting career. He died only seven months later.

Remarkably, although the Ashdown was situated in a dingy street in Islington, it enjoyed the patronage of wealthy members of the aristocracy who, despite the squalor of the locality, enjoyed watching boxing and wrestling matches at the club. In fact, Preedy had named the club after Ashdown Park at Shrivenham, near Swindon, the seat of his close friend and faithful supporter the Earl of Craven. The earl's uncle, the Hon. Osbert W. Craven, was the club's president. It says much about the regard in which Preedy was held by all levels of society, and the high degree of respectability he had established for the club, that members of the upper class felt safe to go there.

Interestingly, Preedy himself acquired something of a reputation as a boxer. Although only 5 feet 5 inches tall, his stocky build and steely eyes gave him a formidable appearance, and none of the neighbourhood toughs would dare raise a finger to him. He used his boxing skills to good advantage in combating the drinking excesses of some of the men of the district. It was said that he had the window of his study specially constructed as a bay so that he could see the White Lion and the Three Johns, pubs that stood at either end of White Lion Street. If a wife reported to him that her husband had been seen entering one of those pubs, Preedy was quickly after him. The fearless cleric had no hesitation in putting up his fists to ensure that the contents of the weekly wage packet were not squandered on drink.

In an interview with *The Sportsman*, Preedy explained how he combined religion and sport at the mission hall:

Without giving the slightest offence, you can call ours the 'Costers' Club' . . . These are the men who would a short time ago have ridiculed the thought of darkening the doors of a church, but who are, by degrees, learning self-respect and realizing that the Divine Master is their friend, and that true religion can be brought into their lives without spoiling their sport and pleasures. The Coster Club membership has grown by leaps and bounds, and it is quite a common sight to see 100 to 150 of them on Tuesday and Wednesday nights boxing and wrestling and thoroughly enjoying themselves in these manly sports. What is more gratifying to me is to see these same men voluntarily coming to their class in church on Sunday afternoons. They love the hymn singing, and though the volume of voice may not be musical, it is nevertheless most hearty.

For Preedy sport and church were not mutually exclusive spheres of life. At the conclusion of each big boxing event he would reinforce this in the minds of the men who attended the club by calling out a reminder to them about the next morning's seven o'clock service in church.

It was not just for the men of the neighbourhood that Preedy provided recreation as a means of welcome relief from the dreariness of life in the slums. He also cared deeply for the girls and women who sold flowers in the street. In the daytime he would invite them into the mission hall to take a break from their work. He would play the piano for them so that they could dance to the music and, for a short while, forget the world outside. An interesting report in the *Morning Leader* with the headline ISLINGTON CLERIC WHO COMBINES DANCING AND DIVINITY captures the spirit of Preedy's musical sessions:

> The Rev. Tiverton Preedy . . . is a versatile Churchman. He boxes, he is willing to challenge any young man in his district to a bout with the gloves, and all the flower girls in Islington and Pentonville simply adore 'Father Preedy'.
>
> As a lady representative of the 'Morning Leader' at the Mission Hall watched the merry feet of the flower girls tripping to infectious music, a wan-faced young woman gently plucked at her sleeve. 'Lidy, would yer 'old me biby while I 'ev a dance?'
>
> The baby was, of course, taken over, and was quite good, whilst the mother danced with her friends. To and fro, to and fro, a curious mixture of the Irish jig, the cake-walk, and the can-can, these supple figures danced quicker, more quickly still. The curate at the piano pushed his biretta back and settled down to hard work. And the flying feet went more quickly than ever.
>
> When the music ceased and the girls flocked out into the streets again struggling to sell their wares, it was easy to explain their affection for Father Preedy.

On 20 May 1926 Preedy received a letter from the Bishop of London which began, 'I should like to recognize your long and faithful work in a poor part of Islington and write to offer you the vacant Prebendal Stall at St Paul's.' It was a great honour to be invited to become a Prebendary of St Paul's Cathedral but when the news got out in the neighbourhood of the All Saints Mission that Preedy had been offered such a position, the residents were devastated. They believed that he would have to leave the area. However, when they learnt that Preedy's acceptance of the position would not prevent him from continuing to live in Islington and ministering at the mission, there was great relief and rejoicing.

Preedy's continuing link with Barnsley FC

Despite Preedy's total commitment to the people he served in Islington, he never forgot Barnsley or Barnsley Football Club. Every Saturday during the football season he would give one of the boys from the neighbourhood a few coppers to buy from a street vendor the late edition of the newspaper, containing the football results. Preedy would eagerly scan them to look for Barnsley's result. It must have given him great pleasure to observe the progress of the club he had founded. The season after he left the town, the club entered the prestigious FA Cup competition for the first time. The team did not progress beyond the first qualifying round, but the following season, 1894–95, they battled through the four qualifying rounds to reach the first round proper. It was a great achievement for a small club. As an indication of St Peter's FC's growing strength and ambition, the club joined the Midland League in the 1895–96 season and the Yorkshire League in 1897–98. The following season, 1898–99, now known as Barnsley Football Club, they became members of the Second Division of the country's top league, the Football League.

Preedy watched these developments with great interest and no doubt with great pride. He also maintained contact with the club as much as possible. If Barnsley should be playing in London he would go along to the match if he could, and he took great delight in meeting old friends who had travelled down. He would then invite them back to his mission where they could enjoy the Saturday night boxing contests. Preedy also occasionally travelled up to Barnsley, especially for important cup games. Right up until his death in 1928 he sent a telegram of encouragement to the Barnsley team before every cup match.

The club's first real taste of glory was the FA Cup Final appearance against Newcastle United at Crystal Palace in 1910. After a 1–1 draw, the replay was lost 2–0 at Everton. But without doubt Preedy's proudest moment in his long association with the club was the Cup Final triumph against West Bromwich Albion in 1912, a feat that earned the club the nickname of 'Battling Barnsley' because of the hard manner in which success was achieved. The team played 12 games to win the trophy, six of which were 0–0 draws and five wins by a narrow one-goal margin. Even the final was a long drawn-out affair, the first match resulting in a 0–0 draw and the winning goal in the replay only coming in the last minute of extra time. Preedy was a guest of the club at both matches, first at the Crystal Palace ground, then at Bramall Lane, Sheffield.

It is not hard to imagine how proud and delighted he must have felt at the team's victory after such a long and gruelling campaign. He must have felt equally proud and delighted when the ball from the replay was presented to him as a mark of the club's affection and esteem. Preedy proudly displayed the ball on a stand in his study in White Lion Street, Islington, until the day he died. It was one of countless souvenirs of the club that crowded his study, but it was the most treasured. After his death in 1928 the ball was returned to Barnsley, bequeathed to the club by Preedy in his will.

At the banquet held to celebrate the Cup Final triumph, Preedy was loudly cheered when he said: 'I was not astonished. We set out to win it, and meant to win it.' He then set the club another goal: 'See to it that we get into the First Division next year. If you cannot do it next year, see that you do it the next . . . Be determined not to rest until you are at the top of the tree.' Stirring words, and ones that were sincerely meant by the man who had nurtured the club in its infancy and proudly watched it grow to maturity.

The death and legacy of Preedy

Although Barnsley was always to be a part of him, Preedy remained in Islington for the rest of his life. He never married. All his time and energies were devoted to the care of the people of the district whom he faithfully served to the very end. In turn he was deeply loved and greatly revered by them. In the last year of his life he suffered from severe heart problems, but he worked on regardless until his body could take no more. He finally succumbed at 6 a.m. on Wednesday 25 April 1928, dying peacefully in his sleep at his home at 90 White Lion Street. He was 65. His years of hard service had finally taken their toll. The report of his death in the *Islington Gazette* of 27 April 1928 gives a clear indication of his determination to continue serving his parishioners, even though the end was very near:

> There can be no doubt that his strenuous work in the past few years, during which the Mission buildings were completely rebuilt, considerably taxed his strength, but nothing would induce him to relax his efforts in the slightest degree. Indeed, he may be said to have died in harness, for on the night preceding his death, he visited the Girls' Club, watched the boys at work in their boxing and gymnastic clubs, and 'listened in' for a few minutes at the Men's Club.

His funeral service took place a few days later on Monday 30 April. It was conducted by the Bishop of Stepney in the mission hall in White Lion Street. The *Islington Gazette* of 1 May describes the occasion vividly: 'Some time before the service began the Mission Church was crowded to overflowing, and hundreds of people sought in vain for admission. It was a most impressive service, and those who remained outside reverently took up the strains of the Easter hymns which were sung. The Bishop of Stepney's touching reference to Father Preedy brought tears to many eyes.' In his address the bishop told the congregation 'You have had a great man in your midst, you have had a wonderful parish priest, and a splendid friend' and he went on to highlight one of Preedy's outstanding gifts, one that had shaped his ministry in both Barnsley and Islington: 'Father Preedy was a sportsman. He could talk to sportsmen. They and he knew that the real power of Father Preedy was his simple, natural, child-like love of the Lord Jesus Christ.'

The mission hall could only hold 200, but it is a mark of the deep affection and great respect felt for Preedy that many thousands lined the streets to say their goodbyes as the cortège made its way to Islington Cemetery. And not a single costermonger's stall was set up in the district that day.

What was it that made Preedy so special to so many people? Why did he attract such devotion? Some idea can be gained from these words in the *Islington Gazette*:

> Father Preedy was devoted to his people and they were devoted to him. He was a generous friend to the poor, often rendering practical assistance when times were particularly hard. By reason of his essentially human personality, Father Preedy gathered about him large numbers of young people who came to look upon him as a tried and trusted friend and one whose advice . . . could be absolutely relied upon.

Truly, Tiverton Preedy was a remarkable man. The selfless life he lived in the service of the underprivileged left a deep impression on countless people in the deprived parish of St Peter's in Barnsley and in the squalid slums of Islington. But he also left his mark on the world of sport. More than 75 years after his death and more than 100 years after he had left St Peter's to pursue his ministry in London, his name is still remembered with affection in Barnsley as the founder of the town's famous football club.

3

Birmingham City

On 18 July 1876 at Holy Trinity Church in the Bordesley district of Birmingham, 21-year-old William Henry Edmonds, an accountant, married his 20-year-old bride, Sarah Allender. The service was conducted by the vicar of Holy Trinity, the Reverend Richard Enraght. Together, Edmonds and Enraght were to make this church famous, but for completely different reasons. Edmonds was one of the members of the choir who created a football club at Holy Trinity from which Birmingham City would eventually emerge. At the same time as the football club was finding its feet, Enraght was at the centre of events that would propel the church into the national limelight. It is a most unusual story.

Holy Trinity Church and the arrival of Richard Enraght

At a meeting at the Bull's Head Inn, Camp Hill, on 4 November 1818 residents of the Bordesley area decided their community needed its own church. They set up a committee to help fund the project and two years later the foundation stone was laid. Building work took about two and a half years but on 23 January 1823 the church, spacious enough to seat a congregation of 1,650, was at last opened for worship. It had been a long but worthwhile wait. The new church was a majestic building of great architectural beauty, the magnificent rose window at the choir end being one of its outstanding features. Situated at the top of Camp Hill with a commanding view of the surrounding countryside in which it then stood, Holy Trinity's lofty position added to its grandeur.

After starting life as a subsidiary of Aston Parish Church in the charge of a curate, Holy Trinity became a parish church in its own right in 1841. That year, Dr Joseph Oldknow was appointed its first vicar. Oldknow served Holy Trinity devotedly for 33 years until his death in 1874 and was succeeded by Richard Enraght, an Irishman born in 1835 who was a graduate of Trinity College, Dublin. He is reputed to have had a brilliant mind. When Enraght arrived at Holy Trinity, it had ceased to be a rural parish. As a result of Birmingham's rapid development as a major industrial city, housing had encroached almost to the church's doorstep and the population of the parish had soared.

Enraght worked hard for his ever-growing number of parishioners. He was an outward-looking and energetic vicar and he encouraged numerous activities that enriched the spiritual and social life of the church. These ranged from Bible classes and prayer meetings to a choral society, a dramatic society, a games club for the over 18s and two libraries. But he was also anxious to address some of the social problems in the area, including poverty and drink. The church set up a soup kitchen for the poor and a volunteer group called the Dorcas Society made clothing for them. A temperance club offered a range of wholesome recreational activities as an alternative to the public house.

The birth of Small Heath Alliance Football Club

In 1871 members of the choir formed a cricket club at the church with the approval of the vicar at the time, Dr Oldknow. Oldknow gave permission for the club to use the church's name in its title and to play as Holy Trinity Cricket Club. When Richard Enraght took over from Oldknow, he was more than happy for this arrangement to continue. The cricketers were a tightly knit group and they enjoyed their summer pastime together, but they were also keen to do something in the winter. By 1875 the relatively new sport of Association football was beginning to become known in the Birmingham area, and in the autumn of that year six of the cricketers – William ('Billy') Edmonds and the brothers Will, Tom and George Edden, and Tom and Fred James – thought it would be a useful activity to take up in the winter months. Apart from the fun of playing, it would also be a useful means of keeping fit. They decided to form a football club but realized that the church alone could not provide enough players familiar with the game to form a team. In order to broaden the club's appeal, they incorporated the name of the wider locality – Small

Heath – into its title and called it 'Small Heath Alliance'. These six enterprising Holy Trinity choristers had just taken a major step towards the creation of the future Birmingham City FC.

Edmonds, although not the eldest of the six, seems to have been their leader and he was appointed the club's first secretary and elected its first captain. Born on 8 September 1854 at 198 Irving Street, not far from Birmingham city centre, he was 21 when Small Heath Alliance was formed. His father, Robert, was a merchant clerk and, like his father, young Edmonds worked as a clerk, initially with a firm of accountants, before starting up his own accountancy business. Prior to his marriage to Sarah Allender, he lived in Cattell Road, a short distance from Holy Trinity and almost next to Birmingham City's present home, St Andrew's. He and Sarah then moved to 178 Camp Hill, in the very shadow of Holy Trinity Church.

The three Edden brothers, like their father, Thomas, were all brick-layers. The eldest of them, William ('Will'), was born on 11 February 1850 and was 25 when the football club was formed. Will was married at Holy Trinity in 1874, the same year that Richard Enraght arrived, although Enraght himself did not conduct the wedding service. When they helped start the club, Will's brothers George and Tom were 21 and 19 respectively and living at home with their parents in Mount Pleasant, a few minutes' walk from Holy Trinity.

Tom and Fred James were originally from Rotherham in Yorkshire where Tom was born in 1855 and Fred four years later in 1859. The James family moved to Birmingham in the early 1860s in search of better work opportunities and both Tom and Fred became fender fitters in the brass industry. Of the six founders of Small Heath Alliance, Fred James was the youngest, being only 16 at the time of the club's formation. The name James was to become well known in Birmingham football circles, not because of Tom or Fred but because of the outstanding talent of their brother, Arthur, who joined the club a year after it was formed. Arthur's skilful play thrilled the crowds of the day and he scored some unforgettable goals. More will be heard of Arthur later.

It is hardly surprising that the founders were such a tightly knit group: all attended Holy Trinity Church, all sang in the choir and all of them lived in close proximity to each other. In 1881 Will Edden was in Cooksey Road a few doors away from Tom James, while George Edden and Fred James lived on opposite sides of Bordesley

Park Road. Tom Edden was their close neighbour in the next street, Mount Pleasant.

The first matches

Of course, the first requirement for the newly formed club was to find somewhere to play. Conveniently, there was an area of open land with a reasonable grass surface in Arthur Street, very close to where they all lived and only a short walk from Holy Trinity Church. Small Heath Alliance's historic first match took place at Arthur Street on a bitterly cold November afternoon in 1875. It was a friendly against Holte Wanderers, a club from the Aston district. It finished in a 1–1 draw, David Keys scoring for Small Heath. Will Edden was in goal that day and the outfield players were Arthur Wright, Fred James, Tom James, George Edden, Billy Edmonds (captain), Tom Edden, David Keys, Charlie Barmore, Clifford Barr and Jack Sparrow. However, when it was discovered in the course of the game that Holte were fielding 12 players, R. Morris was immediately brought on for Small Heath to make the numbers even.

In the close season, club captain Billy Edmonds and his bride were married at Holy Trinity and no doubt Edmonds' team-mates shared their happy day. Three months later the season began with Small Heath Alliance playing at their new home ground in Ladypool Road, Sparkbrook. The first match played there was against Wednesbury Old Park on 7 October 1876 and it was marked by the debut of 19-year-old Arthur James. The game was played 12-a-side and resulted in a 1–0 defeat for Small Heath. As the season progressed, largely due to the presence of James in the side, the team's standard of play improved and they began to attract a following. One notable match was the 4–0 home win against Harborne on 17 March 1877 in which James scored what was probably the club's first hat-trick.

On 11 September 1877 the club moved to Muntz Street, the third ground in its short history. This marked the end of their early nomadic period; it was to remain their home for another 29 years until 1906 when they moved to St Andrew's, their present home. It proved to be a remarkable first season at Muntz Street. Not one of the 22 games played was lost and there were some outstanding victories, including 8–0 against Coventry, 9–0 against Lion Works and the 10–0 hammering of both Walsall Swifts and St Luke's. Some of the stars of the team were Will Edden, who was outstanding in goal, and Clifford Barr, Tom Edden and Jack Sparrow who scored most of the 108 goals. But it was the scintillating play of Arthur James on the right wing that really caught the eye. He was proving to be the dynamo behind the club's success.

Disturbing developments at Holy Trinity

While things could not have been better on the pitch, events were beginning to unfold behind the scenes at Holy Trinity that would send shock waves throughout the nation. Whereas Easter 1878 marked the climax of a highly successful season for Billy Edmonds and his friends, it was the start of a long period of pain and distress for their vicar, Richard Enraght, who was to become the victim of a carefully planned conspiracy.

The trouble began with the vestry meeting on Easter Tuesday when Holy Trinity's two churchwardens (the representatives of the people of the parish) were elected. In accordance with the usual practice, the vicar nominated his choice for the position of Vicar's Warden while the choice of People's Warden was put to a vote by a show of hands. The vote for People's Warden was won by a substantial majority by John Perkins. Unknown to all present, however, Perkins was assured of victory because he had the support of a large number of people, unconnected with Holy Trinity, who had infiltrated the meeting. Why was Perkins so anxious to obtain the position that he was willing to cheat in the election? Because he wanted to use the power granted to individual churchwardens by an Act of Parliament in 1874 – the year Enraght arrived at Holy Trinity – to begin legal proceedings against a vicar who did not conduct Anglican church services in a certain way.

The Act in question was the Public Worship Regulation Act, which outlawed the use of specified practices and rituals of Roman Catholic origin in services of the Church of England. Perkins was an extremist and a member of a vigilante group who aimed to stop 'Ritualist' practices, as they called them. The group often resorted to devious tactics, not only infiltrating churchwarden elections to get their candidate appointed, but also using paid spies to track down Ritualist clergymen. Perkins accused Enraght of being a Ritualist, claiming that his services were not properly conducted in accordance with the rules of the Church of England. Ironically, Billy Edmonds and his friends in the football club who were members of the choir would have taken an active part in these services.

Immediately after his appointment as churchwarden, Perkins started a campaign to discredit Enraght. He organized a series of inflammatory meetings, circulated abusive literature and posted placards in the area. He then contacted the head of the diocese, the Bishop of Worcester, with a list of complaints about the way Enraght was conducting the communion service, although many of the points he listed were actually lies. The bishop dismissed most of them but wrote to Enraght pointing out that four of the practices he had adopted in services were illegal and that he had to stop them. After discussion and an exchange of correspondence with the bishop that lasted well over a year, Enraght finally agreed to his request. The bishop considered it the end of the matter and on 12 July 1879 wrote to Perkins to say the situation was now resolved. Perkins, however, had already started legal proceedings against Enraght and even though the bishop asked him to stop them in the interests of 'the peace of the parish', Perkins refused.

On Saturday 9 August 1879 Enraght was sent for trial but he would not defend himself before the prosecution, stating that he did not recognize the court. He argued that the Public Worship Regulation Act, from which the court derived its authority, had been passed despite the fact that the Church of England parliament (Convocation) had rejected it. He did not feel that the court, a secular authority, had any spiritual jurisdiction over him. Enraght was ruled to be in contempt of court and the charges against him were taken as proved. He was sentenced to prison.

Because of legal wrangling it took more than a year for the sentence to take effect, but finally, on Saturday 27 November 1880, the writ arrived for Enraght's imprisonment in Warwick jail. About 1,000 Holy Trinity parishioners – Billy Edmonds, the Edden and James brothers and other members of the choir almost certainly among them – gathered at the vicarage that day to give him a rousing send-off to Bordesley station from where he would take the train to Warwick.

In the meantime, at the Holy Trinity Easter Vestry of 1880, more than 1,000 parishioners had turned up at the church to vote in the elections for churchwarden. Perkins was nominated by his supporters for re-election but when a count of hands was taken only 15 had been raised in his favour. He immediately demanded a secret ballot to be held there and then, and with Enraght's approval it went ahead. During the counting of the votes Perkins stopped proceedings at the point when he saw that he had registered only 24 votes compared with his rival candidate's 243. He knew there was little point in continuing. He withdrew from the contest and subsequently left the area.

While Enraght was in prison, his numerous supporters worked hard to get the court's decision overturned. Their efforts met with success when the Court of Appeal ruled that he should be released on grounds of a technicality relating to the writ. Enraght left Warwick jail on 17 January 1881 and returned to Holy Trinity, but his story is far from over.

Arthur James, the club's first superstar

During this turbulent period at Holy Trinity, it was business as usual for Edmonds and Small Heath Alliance. In 1878 the club joined the Birmingham & District FA and began to establish itself as one of the foremost in the area. This was due in no small measure to the inspirational play of Arthur James, who had taken over the captaincy from Edmonds at the start of the 1878–79 season. A small stocky figure – he was known as 'Little Arthur' – he was gifted with incredible pace, unerring accuracy and a powerful shot, but he was best known for his skilful dribbling. As one of the outstanding talents in the city, he featured regularly in the Birmingham & District FA representative side in inter-district and inter-county matches, which were only a level below international matches. He was joined in the representative side by goalkeeper Will Edden, who had earned the nickname 'Pouncer' for his goalkeeping style.

The date 27 September 1879 marks an important landmark in Birmingham football when Small Heath Alliance met the renowned Aston Villa for the first time. The game, played at Muntz Street, was the beginning of a long series of derby encounters between the city's two most illustrious clubs. The local press reported that Small Heath won the match by the unusual score of 'one goal and one disputed goal to nil'. In those days 'disputed' goals regularly featured in the scorelines of football matches.

This match marked the start of two seasons of success in friendly matches and by the beginning of the 1881–82 season the club felt it had progressed sufficiently to be able to take part in the prestigious FA Cup competition. They made an excellent start, beating Derby Town 4–1 in the first round before crashing out 6–0 in the second to Wednesbury Old Athletic. Despite the second-round disappointment, it is some measure of how strong a force Small Heath had become in local football that early the following season the club achieved a result that it has never bettered – an 18–1 victory over Elwells from the West Bromwich area.

At the start of the 1882–83 season the club showed its gratitude to Arthur James for the remarkable contribution he had made to its development by presenting him with a gold watch, a cash gift and an illuminated address at the club's annual dinner. On 21 October, a few weeks later, his fortunes took a rapid downward turn when he was badly injured in the match against Druids at Ruabon. It turned out that the injury was so serious that he was laid up for weeks afterwards and the rumour even spread that he had died. A local evening newspaper reported on 11 November that there had been talk of Small Heath Alliance not playing their cup match earlier that day because of the belief that James was dead. Fortunately, it was found that he was alive and afterwards the Birmingham FA voted to send a donation to help him on the road to recovery. It was many months before he was able to play but he never again made the same impact. When he returned to the side in the 1883–84 season, he resumed the captaincy, but his appearances over the next two or three seasons became progressively fewer and he finally retired at the end of the 1886–87 campaign.

Important developments

The injury to Arthur James in 1882 was a real blow to the club, but nevertheless there were also some positive memories that season. The club enjoyed considerable success at its Muntz Street ground and opposing teams dreaded playing there. This was not only due to the quality of Small Heath's play but also to the very bumpy nature of their pitch. When Wednesbury Old Athletic, the holders, were drawn to play there in the Walsall Cup they offered Small Heath £5 to surrender home advantage and play the match at Wednesbury. Small

Heath agreed, accepted the money and duly beat their opponents 4–1. They went on to beat Walsall Swifts away in the final and secure their first-ever trophy. They clearly were not dependent on the advantages that Muntz Street offered.

During the course of the next few seasons, significant changes began to occur off the pitch. At the end of the 1883–84 season Billy Edmonds stood down as secretary after faithfully serving the club in that role for nine years. He was succeeded by Will Edden, who had recently retired as goalkeeper. A year later, in August 1885, there was another change of secretary – Alfred Jones succeeding Will Edden – when the momentous decision was taken to turn professional. This was done mainly because the players could not afford the loss of earnings at work when they took time off to train and play. It was agreed that the players' pay would be in line with gate receipts, half the net takings being shared between them.

The move to professionalism seemed to have a very positive effect on the team: they started the 1885–86 FA Cup campaign with a magnificent 9–2 win against Burton Wanderers and reached the semi-final for the first time in the club's history. It was local rivals West Bromwich who blocked their path to the final. Fred James, the last of the founders still in the team, was later proudly photographed with his semi-final medal.

The next big step in the club's development was the decision taken on 24 July 1888 to become a limited liability company. The 'Alliance' was dropped from its title and it was duly registered under its new name, Small Heath Football Club Limited – the first club in England to become a limited company with a board of directors. The first chairman of the board was Walter Hart, a local businessman, and at the end of the first financial year Hart proudly reported that the club had made a considerable profit and he was in the happy position of being able to pay a five per cent dividend to shareholders.

Ambitions were now growing and, before the start of the 1889–90 season, Small Heath were accepted into membership of the newly created Football Alliance, a strong league with many fine teams. In their first two seasons in the Alliance, Small Heath struggled to find their feet against the better quality opposition they encountered and they finished third from bottom both times. However, their play improved dramatically in 1891–92 when they achieved a third-place finish. It was very good timing because the league was about to be absorbed into the Football League, the best in England, forming its Second Division. It is a measure of how much the team had improved that they finished champions of the Second Division in 1892–93 and although they failed to win promotion in the play-offs, they did not have long to wait before stepping up to the top flight. Brushing aside their earlier disappointment, they made a determined bid for promotion in the next campaign and their efforts were duly rewarded with a second-place finish and success in the play-offs. The club that had started as a humble little church cricket team had now joined the élite of English football.

There were, of course, to be many more important developments, including the change of name to Birmingham in 1905 then Birmingham City in 1946, the move to St Andrew's in 1906, and, in more recent times, promotion to the FA Premier League in 2002. The club was to leave its humble church roots far behind, but the names of Billy Edmonds and his friends who had laid the foundations for Birmingham City's rise to greatness should not be forgotten. They, at least, did not forget the club they had founded and continued to support it for many years after they had stopped playing.

Richard Enraght: the final chapter

On his release from prison, Enraght returned to Holy Trinity as vicar but his days there were numbered. Early in November 1882 the Bishop of Worcester had written to Enraght stating that under the terms of the Public Worship Regulation Act it had been his duty to inform the patrons of Holy Trinity that the position of vicar was due to become vacant. Enraght was about to be dismissed. In a desperate attempt to stop this happening, the churchwardens had appealed to the Bishop of Worcester to reverse the decision on the grounds that the whole prosecution appeared to them to be a conspiracy. On behalf of the parishioners they had also forwarded a resolution to the Queen, the Prime Minister and the Archbishop of Canterbury, among others, urging them to do all they could to prevent Enraght being removed.

But it was no use. On 3 March 1883 Enraght received an official letter stating that his licence had been revoked and that he could no longer practise as a clergyman within the Diocese of Worcester. A few days later, on Sunday 11 March, Enraght's successor, the Reverend

Alan Watts, took his first service at Holy Trinity. Thousands assembled at the church to protest at Enraght's dismissal and such was the
strength of feeling that the police had to be called to keep order. Did
Billy Edmonds and the others take part in this protest?

On 28 March Enraght said farewell to his parishioners at a crowded meeting in a local school. There was great sadness at his leaving
and he received many tributes. The chairman of the meeting told
the audience that Enraght was 'a man whose standard of goodness
it was hard to reach' and that he had earned 'the esteem and love of
his people'. A tribute also appeared in *The Guardian* in which it
was stated that 'The people . . . have learnt to love and respect Mr
Enraght, who has laboured in his parish with unwearied kindness,
and to value the many agencies for good which had grown up
under his ministry.' The cricket club formed by his choristers was
just one of the 'agencies for good' that Enraght had supported.

On leaving Holy Trinity, Enraght and his wife moved to Brighton
where Enraght had served as a curate prior to coming to Birmingham.
They subsequently moved to a country parish in Norfolk where
Enraght died in 1898 at the age of 63. His obituary in a Birmingham
newspaper mentioned that he 'never overgot the strain of that trying
time'. The events that caused Enraght such distress are now long past
but he and the other clergymen in England who were imprisoned as
a result of the Public Worship Regulation Act are still remembered in
some quarters as 'The Victorian Martyrs'.

Continuing church and sport links in Birmingham

Holy Trinity was a focus of sports activities for a good many years.
Apart from the cricket and football clubs formed by members of
the choir in the 1870s, there was also a thriving athletics club in the
1890s. And interestingly, the vicar of Holy Trinity from 1911 to 1914,
the Reverend F. H. Gillingham, was a county cricketer. But Holy
Trinity was not the only church in Birmingham that encouraged
sport. In fact, about a quarter of all the football clubs founded in the
city between 1876 and 1884 were of church origin.

Sporting links with churches in the Birmingham area were still
strong in 1925. A footballers' service, for example, was held at Christ
Church in West Bromwich and was attended by members of prominent local clubs including West Bromwich Albion and Birmingham

City. Among the players present were James Spencer, the Albion outside-right who read the lesson, and Birmingham City's captain, Frank Womack.

Holy Trinity once again made the news in 1950 when a series of recitals by the choir and organist was begun in November to raise money for essential repair work to the church. The 1950 choir, like that in which Billy Edmonds and his friends had sung, seemed to enjoy the combination of singing and play. After their evening practice the boys would make their way to a room set aside for them to enjoy table tennis, darts and snooker in their own Choirboys' Club. Enraght would no doubt have been delighted. But sadly, at the time of writing, there is no choir, no vicar and no congregation at Holy Trinity. The majestic building astride Camp Hill now stands empty. Perhaps as Birmingham City supporters catch a glimpse of the church on their way home from the ground, they might think for a moment about the important part it has played in their great club's history.

4

Bolton Wanderers

———•◦•———

At the start of Deane Road, Bolton, immediately in front of a small grassed area with a few untidy flowerbeds, stands a rusty and badly damaged sign. It struggles to inform passers-by that they have arrived at Christ Church Gardens, although there is little to entice them to stop here. The gardens themselves lack any real beauty and the view they enjoy of a car park immediately across the road is hardly breathtaking. Yet this was the setting for the foundation of one of England's great football clubs – Bolton Wanderers. It is hard to imagine today that on the site of the gardens once stood an Anglican church called Christ Church, while across the road on the car park stood a building that housed two Christ Church schools, one for boys, the other for girls. It was in this building in 1874 that the vicar of Christ Church, the Reverend Joseph Wright, persuaded the headmaster of the boys' school, Thomas Ogden, to start up a football club for members of the church Sunday School. It was to become famous.

The founders of the club

Christ Church, built in 1818, was originally a Methodist chapel but it passed into the hands of the Church of England in 1841 when it became the parish church of a poor and deprived district. The majority of the parishioners earned very low wages in local factories and mills: it was not uncommon to find whole families living in a single room in many of the back-to-back terraced houses that dominated the area. It was here that Joseph Farrall Wright arrived in 1871 to become the new vicar of Christ Church.

Wright was born in Manchester in 1827. After training for the Anglican ministry at St Bee's College, Cumberland, he was ordained a deacon in 1851. He then served as a curate at St Philip's, Sheffield, and at Christ Church, Stone, in Staffordshire, before coming to Bolton in

1860 on a dual appointment as assistant curate and lecturer at St Peter's Church. While serving at St Peter's, Wright lived at 25 Silverwell Street in a six-bedroomed Georgian terraced house in a fashionable quarter of the town with his wife, Harriet, their daughter and their three sons. But increasingly he became aware of a call to the poor and deprived. Finally, in 1871, certain of his call, he accepted the offer of the position of vicar of Christ Church and so, at the age of 44, he moved with his wife and children into this needy parish.

Despite his certainty that he was called to Christ Church, it could not have been easy for Wright to leave St Peter's. According to *The Bolton Evening Guardian* he had established very close ties with the parishioners there, having 'earned the respect of all with whom he came in contact, alike for his faithfulness to duty and his general courtesy'. He had also become very involved with the work of the Sunday School, whose teachers and pupils had developed a deep affection for him. He knew they did not want him to go, but he was convinced that the time was right for him to leave.

Wright remained at Christ Church for the rest of his life. As at St Peter's, he established strong bonds of affection with the people he served. *The Bolton Journal* reports that he came to be regarded by them as 'a true friend and a loving minister'. Although 'firm in principles, fearless in action' he built happy, harmonious relationships within the church in a quiet, unostentatious manner. Ever mindful of the needs of the underprivileged, he became a committed and industrious member of the Bolton Poor Protection Society, working tirelessly for this organization for many years and eventually becoming its secretary. He regularly visited the homes of the poor and he gave help wherever he could.

But Wright also had a deep concern for young people and he was a frequent visitor to the three Christ Church schools (boys', girls' and infants'). He encouraged his sister, Mary, and his second wife, Ellen (whom he married in 1876 after the death of Harriet in 1874), to assist in the girls' and infants' schools with reading and sewing and to listen to the children sing. Mary, in particular, was a very regular visitor and she would give the children sweets, apples and oranges, while Wright himself is known to have distributed buns and coffee in the girls' school and to have organized a party for them there. An entry in the infants' school logbook for 7 July 1882 gives some indication of the Wright family's concern for the poor children of the district. It is recorded that a boy who had been playing truant returned to school 'barefoot, ragged and very dirty and Mrs Wright took him, washed and clothed him, and he has been very good since'. Wright had a particularly close involvement with the boys' school, visiting it on a regular basis, and it was his association with the head-master, Thomas Ogden, that led to the birth of Bolton Wanderers.

Tom Ogden was a local man, born in Kearsley, Bolton, on 18 January 1846. His father worked in the textile industry as a self-employed fly and spindle maker but Tom chose not to follow in his father's footsteps, preferring instead to become a teacher. He followed the usual path of teacher training at the time, progressing from a monitor (a pupil who passed on the teacher's instruction to other pupils), to teacher-pupil (a trainee serving a five-year classroom apprenticeship from age 13 to 18), to college student. On 11 January 1869, exactly one week before his twenty-third birthday, Ogden was appointed headmaster of Christ Church Boys' School. It was to prove a very tough assignment.

Christ Church Boys' School, the club's first HQ

Ogden could not have arrived at a worse time. He was the sole teacher for some 140 pupils and he had to teach them all simultaneously in the school hall with the help of a single monitor. His problems were many. Absenteeism and truancy were rampant, punctuality was dreadful, and disobedience and misbehaviour frequently reared their ugly heads. Furthermore, it was not helpful that young hooligans roamed the area seeking to disrupt lessons. He could not even count on parents for support. Some of them actively encouraged truancy so that their children could supplement the family income by finding casual work in one of the local textile mills.

There was added discouragement only five months after his arrival. Following an inspection by one of Her Majesty's Inspectors, the school received a damning report in which it was stated that 'the discipline and general efficiency of the school is much below the mark'. The government grant to the school was reduced by one-tenth with the threat of a further reduction if there was not a marked improvement the next year. Perhaps the fact that the report recog-nized the shortage of staff was some consolation to Ogden and as he was due to get the services of an assistant master any day, he had reasonable grounds for optimism. But they proved to be misplaced. Only two months or so after taking up his appointment, Ogden's assistant handed in his notice on the grounds of poor pay. Ogden was back to where he had started. Not surprisingly, he frantically began to advertise in the local papers and in a teachers' journal for a replacement, but to no avail. No one, it seemed, wanted to work in this tough area.

Although another assistant was eventually recruited in January 1870, he, too, did not last long, resigning after only three months. The problems seemed to be never-ending. Ogden's logbook gives some indication of his struggles at the time: 'Many boys late – a great fault, tried various means to "cure"', 'Sent after absentees', 'Boys working unsatisfactorily', 'Spoke to some boys for rudeness', and the cryptic remark 'A mother came to enquire about her boy being punished'.

The Wright–Ogden partnership

There was a lot of work to be done and Ogden was quite prepared to do it. He was a dedicated teacher and with the help of one or two monitors he slowly and painfully began to turn things round. Remarkably, in view of the difficulties that Ogden had encountered in his first year, the inspector was able to write in the 1870 inspection report that 'The tone of this school has improved and to some extent the attainments.' Ogden battled on and within another year the attainments, too, had improved, the inspector reporting that 'The boys have passed a satisfactory examination in the elementary subjects.' But the real turning point came when the Revd Joseph Wright was appointed vicar of Christ Church in 1871. Wright and Ogden were to form a partnership that would not only transform the school but also lead to the creation of a major new football club in the town.

With Wright behind him, Ogden was able to take the school forward in spectacular fashion. Although assistant masters continued to come and go with alarming regularity, Ogden achieved remarkable success. The first major breakthrough came with the 1872 inspection report: 'The order is good, the extra subjects were well done and the results of the examination gave proofs of careful teaching.' And this was confirmed in 1873 when the report read 'The order is good and the boys are taught with much vigour and success.' The Wright–Ogden partnership was obviously working and it is perhaps appropriate that when Ogden married Ann Markland, the 24-year-old daughter of a Bolton butcher, on 30 July 1873 at Holy Trinity Church, it was the Revd Joseph Wright who conducted the ceremony.

A year later, in 1874, Wright and Ogden held a conversation that was to have remarkable consequences. Despite the considerable age difference between them – Wright was 47, Ogden 28 – the two men had clearly developed a good understanding and worked well together as a team. One particular interest they shared was sport. Ogden was a football enthusiast, having learned to play a form of the game at college. Wright, on the other hand, though not an active sportsman himself, was influenced by the 'muscular Christian' belief, popular in many churches, that team sports such as cricket and football were healthy pastimes that developed qualities of character such as courage, self-control, fair play and unselfishness. He was intrigued to discover that a new variety of football had recently been introduced in the neighbouring village of Turton and knowing that Ogden was a frequent visitor there, he asked him to investigate. Wright wondered if this new form of the game might be something that the young men of the Christ Church Sunday School could enjoy.

The birth of the club

Ogden set off to examine the Turton brand of football. He was unsure of what he would find as there were so many versions of the game in England, each with a different set of rules. When the Turton club was founded in 1871 by John Charles Kay, it initially played according to the rules of Harrow School where Kay had been a pupil. The club continued to play by the Harrow rules until 1874 but then switched to 'soccer'. This version of football had begun to spread throughout England, but Turton had the distinction of being the first club in Lancashire to take it up. Other clubs soon followed but in the meantime the Turtonians were happy to play matches among themselves by Association rules. Ogden was thoroughly impressed by the Harrow version of the game that he witnessed at Turton and he gave an enthusiastic account of it to the Revd Wright. It did not take them long to decide that a football club should be formed at Christ Church and that Harrow rules should be adopted.

Sometime in June 1874 Ogden called a meeting at his school of young men who attended the church Sunday School and were interested in the idea of forming a church club. As they were unfamiliar with the Harrow game, Ogden knew that he had to convince them of its merits. But probably due to his infectious enthusiasm and the respect he had earned as headmaster, he had little difficulty in winning them over and it was quickly agreed that a club should be formed. The decision was then taken that it should be called Christ Church Football Club, with the vicar of Christ Church, the Revd Wright, as its president. The Christ Church Boys' School (where the Sunday School met) was to be its headquarters. Tom Ogden was appointed captain and Tom Rawsthorne secretary. Others who were also present at that historic meeting were Tom Rawsthorne's brothers, John and Robert, Joe Boardman, Charles Cooper, Jonathan Garside and Tom Naylor. It was agreed that sixpence should be collected from each member for the purchase of a football and, additionally, that there should be a membership fee of one penny per week.

The first matches

The youthful enthusiasts were eager to get started and they arranged to play a practice match on the first Saturday in July. They were given permission to use a field which was then known as 'Bob Wood's' but now forms part of Heaton Cemetery. To the players' great disappointment, the match could not take place that day because of terrible weather. However, conditions were more favourable the following Saturday and so the game went ahead. It quickly became obvious that these raw recruits needed to work hard at developing their skills, which were rudimentary to say the least. Ogden, who was not without ability, was able to coach them to some extent but he felt they needed to learn from the experts. And the experts were Turton FC, the best exponents of the game locally. It was therefore arranged that the members of the Christ Church club should watch the Turtonians in action and pick up some useful tips from them.

The Christ Church club's first match was in 1874 against Farnworth at Smithfield, a field off Plodder Lane. Although the result is not known it seems that one half of the game was played according to Association rules, the other according to Rugby rules. Clearly, football clubs were still finding their way and as no one particular code was widely established at the time, compromises had to be made when clubs played each other. Christ Church matches in the early years tended to be against other Sunday School teams that had sprung up in Bolton and its neighbouring villages. As it was mostly churches that provided recreation for young people in late Victorian times (in the same way that youth clubs do today) it is perhaps not surprising that almost a quarter of all clubs founded in England at the time were named after churches.

In the beginning Christ Church FC had no ground of their own and played wherever they could. Several different fields were used until they made the municipal recreation ground their base. Of course, as the recreation ground was a public park there was no guarantee that a preferred pitch would always be available, since other clubs also played there. And so, with a desire for greater independence, the club took the decision to rent a field known as 'Dick Cockle's' on Pike's Lane. It was to be the last ground at which the team played under the name of Christ Church Football Club.

The split with the church

All had gone well for three years until one eventful day in 1877 when there was a serious disagreement between the president, the Revd Wright, and the club committee. Wright took his role as president very seriously and did not consider himself to be simply a figurehead. He took an active part in all the club's affairs and attended all committee meetings. In fact, he considered these meetings to be so important that he would not allow them to take place if he was unable to be present. It caused considerable tension within the club. Wright probably felt that he had to safeguard the good name of his church as it featured so prominently in the club's title, and that the best way to do this was to keep a watchful eye on all club developments, including decisions taken at committee meetings. The members of the committee, on the other hand, considered him to be intrusive and his attitude to be authoritarian. In consequence, they rebelled and decided to part company with him and his church.

This may have been a somewhat impetuous move. After all, Wright was not known in the parish to be authoritarian. Indeed, it is difficult to understand how a man who was widely regarded as 'a true friend and a loving minister', who was always courteous, and who went about things quietly and unostentatiously should fall foul of the very people he had wanted to help. It was he, after all, who had urged Ogden to form a football club for them. Perhaps the club had begun to recruit from outside the Sunday School and unwholesome influences of some kind were beginning to creep into it? Perhaps club funds were not being used wisely enough? It is very hard to believe that Wright wanted to be present at every committee meeting without good reason.

A new name and new leaders

But the decision to leave Christ Church had been taken and new headquarters had to be found. The school would no longer be available. Happily, the club's search for a new home did not last long as the Gladstone Hotel not far from their pitch in Pike's Lane was able to provide a new base. There was now the important question of a new name. This was a key topic for discussion at the committee's last meeting at the Christ Church Boys' School on 28 August 1877 and it did not take the members long to think of one. Prompted by the fact that the club had had to 'wander' in search of new headquarters, the committee decided that the its new name should be Bolton Wanderers.

The break with Christ Church placed Tom Ogden in an impossible situation. He obviously loved the club that Wright had encouraged him to form, and of which he was captain, but he also had loyalties to his vicar and the church. And, needless to say, his position as headmaster of Christ Church Boys' School would have been untenable had he joined the rebels. He felt he had no option but to leave the club. With both Wright and Ogden gone, it fell to members of the Rawsthorne family to assume control. Tom continued as secretary (a position he held until 1885), Robert took over as captain and William, their father, who had actively supported the club since its inception, succeeded Wright as president.

Ironically, in view of the complaint that Wright was too authoritarian, William Rawsthorne ran the club with a rod of iron. He drew up the club rules and insisted that they be upheld. He immediately introduced fines for swearing, for failure to attend meetings and for failure to inform the secretary in good time of inability to play in a match. When printed copies of the rules were made available to the club members in September 1878, Rawsthorne fined anyone who lost his copy. Was it a case of out of the frying pan into the fire for those who had been disgruntled with Wright?

Another significant development occurred in 1878 when Peter Parkinson, the manager of a textile mill in the town, became a member of the club. His contribution was immediately felt. As an individual with great drive, energy and ambition he helped establish the club as a force in the area. Within only two or three years of his arrival, Bolton were beating teams of the calibre of Blackburn Olympic, Preston North End and Turton FC, their former tutors. Parkinson became the driving force behind the club and it is no surprise that he was elected president in 1881. He steered Wanderers towards professionalism in 1885 and thus laid the foundation for their admission to the Football League in 1888. There were great days ahead.

The legacy of the club's founders

Unfortunately, neither Wright nor Ogden lived long enough to see the club they had created rise to greatness. In fact, they both died within only a few months of each other. Wright died first. He had suffered a long and painful illness but he continued to serve the impoverished parish of Christ Church for as long as he was physically able. But in his fifty-seventh year, on 19 June 1883 at the vicarage, he finally succumbed to an inflammation of the brain. His final thoughts were of his parishioners, and his last words were 'Tell them, tell them all, that I wish them all God's blessing.' Wright was laid to rest on Saturday 23 June in the churchyard of Christ Church, Walmsley, presumably because the tiny graveyard adjoining his own church was already full.

Wright's link with the club, even after his death, was not totally severed. His care for the poor had always been a key feature of his work in the parish and while he was president of Christ Church FC the club had always made an annual contribution to the funds of the Bolton Poor Protection Society, of which he was secretary. However, even after the parting of the ways between club and church, Bolton Wanderers continued to make its annual contribution to the society until the outbreak of World War I.

Another continuing link between Wright and the club was through his second son, also called Joseph Farrall Wright. Wright junior trained at Manchester University to become a doctor and after gaining his qualifications he returned to Bolton where he joined a medical practice in Deane Road. Young Wright had supported Christ Church FC from the day the club was born – he was only nine years old at the time – and he continued to be a passionate supporter long after it had changed its name to Bolton Wanderers. Such was his enthusiasm for Bolton Wanderers that he not only became a shareholder but also encouraged his junior partner at the Deane Road practice, Dr Cochrane, to become the club doctor and then a director. Wright's father would have been amused by the irony!

Sadly, Tom Ogden, who had formed Christ Church FC, did not enjoy a long life. He lived only until the age of 38, dying at his home at 13 Bertrand Road on 8 March 1884 from a liver abscess. According to the president of the Bolton Teachers' Association, Ogden's death 'was accelerated by overwork and over-anxiety'. There can be little doubt that the 15 years of struggle at the tough Christ Church Boys' School had finally taken their toll. The first real indication that Ogden was suffering from the strain of overwork is evident from the school logbook entry for 5 April 1878: 'The Assistant Master still away. The work of this school is very arduous to the Master [Ogden], he having only the assistance of young pupil-teachers.' Ogden was also clearly frustrated by the lack of support from the local school board in helping him to chase up absentees. His logbook entry for 10 November 1882 makes this abundantly clear when, following the visit of the school board officer, he writes: 'No good will come of it as the Master never hears anything further about the irregulars and has not done so for over 12 months back.'

But in those 15 years of struggle, Ogden rarely missed a day's work. His only recorded absences, until the failure of his health in the last three weeks of his life, were for funerals. He lost his brother, Robert, in March 1876, his father-in-law, William Markland, on 8 January 1879, and then, tragically, only five days later, his eight-month-old daughter, Ida, who died of bronchitis. The year 1879 was one that Ogden was unlikely to forget. In addition to the deaths of his father-in-law and his baby daughter, he also had to endure the loss of his great friend, James Ritson, in November.

It was probably due to his Christian faith that he was able, against all the odds, to achieve so much at the school. There is certainly a strong hint of this in the inspection report of 27 October 1882: 'The school as a whole did well . . . The influences at work in the school seemed to be of a directly religious kind.' But whatever Ogden's achievements as a headmaster – and they are considerable in view of the enormous difficulties he had to face – there can be little doubt that the achievement for which his name will go down in history is the formation of Christ Church Football Club, the forerunner of Bolton Wanderers.

As for Christ Church itself, it was closed in 1933 when a slum clearance programme drastically reduced the number of parishioners in the area and the size of the congregation dwindled accordingly. The building was finally demolished in May 1936 and the site sold to Bolton Corporation in August 1938 for use as a children's play-ground. Eventually, in 1956, the playground was relaid as a public garden and named Christ Church Gardens. The Christ Church school building across the road, like the church itself, was declared redundant when the slum clearance programme reduced the size of the local population. This impressive building, which had housed a boys' school and a girls' school, stood empty and decaying for many years until it too was demolished and the site used for a car park. Perhaps when passers-by see the rusty, damaged sign at the entrance to Christ Church Gardens and glance across the road to the car park they might pause and reflect on the contribution of these now un-remarkable sites to the fame of their town in the world of football.

5

Everton . . . and its offspring Liverpool

In 2003 the Everton club shop introduced a new range of T-shirts, caps and bobble hats. There is nothing particularly remarkable about that because items such as these are a normal feature of club sales. Yet these items were very different. They did not bear the name of Everton but of a totally different football club. So why was the Everton club shop selling T-shirts and headgear with the name 'St Domingo's' emblazoned across them? Quite simply because 2003 was the 125th anniversary of the club's birth and it was honouring the chapel by which it had been founded. These items are still on sale at the club today but they could also be sold with equal justification at the Liverpool FC club shop at Anfield. Because, surprisingly, Everton's great local rivals across Stanley Park can also trace their roots to St Domingo Methodist Chapel. This is a story that must be told.

St Domingo's, the Wades and the Cuffs

The decision to build St Domingo's was taken in 1868 after it had become clear that the numbers attending three other Liverpool chapels belonging to the Methodist New Connexion (one of the branches of Methodism at the time) had dwindled to an unacceptable level. It seemed to make more sense to close the three non-viable chapels and to run a single thriving one. Bethesda, Bevington Hill and Chatham Place chapels were therefore closed and the building of St Domingo's started on 12 September 1870 when 55-year-old Joseph Wade, one of its newly appointed trustees, laid the foundation stone. About a year later, on 20 July 1871, the first services were held there. It is worth mentioning that St Domingo's did not choose its name for any religious reasons. It simply took the name from two parallel streets between which it was situated, St Domingo Grove and St Domingo Vale. It was a predominantly middle-class area.

Joseph Wade, who was given the honour of laying the foundation stone of St Domingo's, was born in 1815 in Halifax. After he married Grace Riley there, the couple, both in their mid-twenties, left Yorkshire for Liverpool where Joseph set up a coach-building business in the then affluent district of Everton. At the time St Domingo's was being built, he was employing 20 men and seven boys. Joseph and Grace had eight children. Their youngest, Alfred Riley Wade, was a member of the first known Everton team and was to become a director of the club in one of the most exciting periods of its history.

It is little surprise that Joseph was invited to lay the foundation stone of the St Domingo Chapel. He had been a highly respected trustee at Bevington Hill Chapel and was a key figure in getting St Domingo's up and running. He helped choose the site for the new chapel at the junction of Breckfield Road North and St Domingo Vale and he was also involved in negotiations for buying the land. Once it had been bought, he was one of the people responsible for all the building arrangements. It was also Wade who secured the purchase of 128 Queen's Road for the minister's home. Furthermore, he was a very generous benefactor of the chapel, donating a considerable amount of money towards its building costs. This stalwart of the chapel died in September 1875 at the age of 60 and, sadly, did not live long enough to see Alfred play in Everton's first match.

The Cuffs were another family who played a hugely important part in the history of both St Domingo's and Everton. Henry Cuff, like Joseph Wade, was appointed a trustee of St Domingo's when it opened and, again like Wade, was a devoted and loyal servant of the chapel until he died. He was born in 1836 in Poplar, London, but later moved to Liverpool where he met his wife, Mary, a girl from Pwllheli, near Caernarfon in North Wales. Cuff opened a pork butcher's shop and by 1881 his business was sufficiently successful for him to be able to afford to employ two servants at the family home at 34 Spellow Lane, just round the corner from Everton's present ground, Goodison Park. Henry and Mary had eight children, four boys and four girls. The second of their children, William, was born on 19 August 1868. Like his father, he was a faithful servant of St Domingo's but he was also to become one of the most respected and influential figures in Everton's history.

There was very little that Henry Cuff did not do for St Domingo's. He was treasurer, he chaired meetings, he was on the Sunday School committee and the organ-building committee, he represented the chapel at outside meetings, he was active in outreach work to the local community and he entertained visitors. No task was beneath him. He was even in charge of removing tables from the tea-room. But he also had great moral authority and he was entrusted with sensitive tasks calling for tact and skill in dealing with others. This ranged from speaking to a member of the chapel about his lack of moral standards to reprimanding the chapel caretaker for the dirty state of the premises. Even after he had moved some considerable distance from Liverpool to Llay, near Wrexham, Henry Cuff continued to take a full part in the work of St Domingo's. After his death in May 1911 at the age of 75, the trustees of the chapel, in the minutes of their meeting of 24 May, paid tribute to his 'character, life and service'.

The founder of the club

The names Cuff and Wade will appear again in this account of the club's history but a name that Evertonians should always remember with gratitude is Ben Swift Chambers, who became the minister of St Domingo Chapel in July 1877. The reason, quite simply, is that he is the founder of their club. Chambers was born on 30 August 1845 at Stocksmoor near Huddersfield. His father, Joah, worked first as a clothier but later switched occupations and became a schoolteacher in Shepley, near Huddersfield, where Ben grew up. Ben (he was not named 'Benjamin' as is often assumed) served an apprenticeship with a high-class engraver in Huddersfield and was so good at his work that his employer offered him a partnership in the business. But young Chambers felt that his calling was to the Methodist ministry. Even at an early age he was teaching in his local church Sunday School. He served his church with such enthusiasm and dedication that its members were certain he would become a minister.

At 22 he began a two-year period of training at the Methodist College and on qualification in 1869 he took up his first appointment as a minister in the Ashton circuit. He served one year in Ashton before spending a year in Stockport and two in Halifax. It was the normal pattern at the time for Methodist ministers to serve only short periods in each circuit. While in Halifax, he married 28-year-old Elizabeth Holden, a farmer's daughter from Shepley, on 9 June 1873. The couple moved the same year to Barrow and after spending two years there and a further two in Gateshead, they finally arrived at St Domingo's. Chambers was now 32.

Chambers quickly established himself at St Domingo's. According to the Methodist New Connexion Conference Minutes of 1902, he possessed 'a powerful and winning personality' and people found themselves easily drawn to him. As the minutes state, he was considered to be a 'manly, affectionate, kindly, pleasant, happy, noble being . . . eager to serve, anxious to do good . . . a never-failing friend'. He was also an excellent communicator who loved preaching. He had a particular concern for the wellbeing of young people, and he became actively involved in initiatives that benefited them educationally and spiritually. At St Domingo's he took a leading part in the Band of Hope group that had been set up to encourage young people to resist the temptation of drink, a major social problem at the time.

The St Domingo Football Club is born

Chambers was a great lover of cricket. Within only a month of arriving in Liverpool, he had persuaded members of the Young Men's Bible Class in the Sunday School, most of them aged about 20, to form a St Domingo's cricket team. And such was Chambers' enthusiasm for the game that he could not resist joining in with them. He didn't know what he had started.

A year later, in 1878, these same cricketers, among them Alfred Wade, felt it would be a good idea to take up football during the long winter months to keep themselves fit. And to give themselves a distinct identity as footballers they decided to call themselves The St Domingo Football Club. The first step had been taken on a road that was to lead to fame and glory.

The youthful St Domingo's enthusiasts had found nearby Stanley Park ideal for cricket and they felt it would serve equally well for football. They chose an area in the south-east corner for their games, probably because it was closest to where they lived. Of course, there were no conveniently marked out pitches with goalposts. If they wanted goalposts, they had to carry them from a lodge in the centre of the park and erect them themselves. Nor did they enjoy the luxury of changing facilities in Stanley Park. But they probably didn't need any because in the very early days they would have just turned up in old clothes.

At first, they played impromptu games between themselves but few passers-by would have been tempted to stand and watch because there was little to see that would have aroused wonder or admiration. Their style of play was very basic, being little more than a furious scramble for possession. However, it did at least enthral one ardent supporter, ten-year-old Will Cuff, son of St Domingo trustee Henry Cuff. Will was a regular spectator and it gave him huge pleasure to watch his older friends from the chapel in action. It was here that football first caught his imagination and this was the starting point in an association with the game that would lead him to its very summit. But there was yet another symbolic presence close by. Overlooking the pitch where the youthful enthusiasts were practising their rudimentary skills stood – and still stands – an imposing building called Stanley House. It was once the home of John Houlding, a local brewer. Much more will be heard of Houlding later. Liverpool supporters might recognize his name . . .

The change of name to Everton

St Domingo's was not the only church team taking its first tentative steps in Stanley Park in 1878–79. A number of others were also playing there, including St Benedict's, St Peter's and the United Church. Church clubs, in fact, were a growing feature of the football landscape in Liverpool and by 1885 some 25 of the 112 clubs playing in the city had connections with religious organizations. After a few practice games among themselves, the St Domingo lads were ready to take on some of the other church teams in the park. They had not yet developed the style of play that would one day earn the club the title 'The School of Science' but they very quickly became the best team in the park. As a result, the better players from the other clubs began to look in their direction.

The club was happy to recruit new talent because it wanted to continue to grow in strength but there was one big problem: the players they were attracting were not members of St Domingo Chapel. Six were from the United Church while a further four came from St Peter's. The club was ceasing to be truly representative of the chapel. By November 1879 this was felt to be an extremely awkward situation and so a meeting was called at the Queen's Head Hotel in Village Street, Everton, not far from St Domingo's, to discuss it. It was decided that the best solution would be a complete change of name. One that quickly suggested itself was the district where most of them lived – Everton. The name was agreed and John Clark, landlord of the Queen's Head, was appointed the club's first official secretary.

Remarkably, no decision was made about the choice of club colours. St Domingo's played in blue and white stripes but it was agreed to let the players who had joined from other clubs continue playing in the strips of their former clubs. Perhaps the cost of buying new ones was considered prohibitive. This situation did not change until October 1881, and in the meantime the Everton team in its variety of colours must have looked quite a sight.

Under its new name, the club got off to the best possible start, handing out a 6–0 thrashing on 23 December 1879 to their local church rivals St Peter's. Unfortunately neither the team line-up nor the names of the goalscorers in that historic match are known but the local press printed the names of the team in the return match against St Peter's on 24 January 1880 in Stanley Park, which resulted in a convincing 4–0 win for Everton. Playing in a 2-2-6 formation, the line-up that day was: W. Jones (goal); T. Evans and J. Douglas (backs); C. Hiles and S. Chalk (capt.) (half-backs); R. W. Morris, A. White, Frank Brettle, Alfred Wade, Smith and W. Williams (forwards). Joseph Wade's son, Alfred, was one of the forwards.

The cricket club continues

It would be interesting to know what happened to the St Domingo's players who were not part of the new set-up. Many of them carried on playing in the original chapel cricket club from which the football club emerged. The club was certainly in existence in the autumn of 1879 as the following intriguing entry in the minutes of the St Domingo Leaders' Meeting of 17 September confirms: 'It was . . . resolved that the application of the St Domingo cricket club for the use of the large [school] room for a concert on the 25 Oct be granted subject to certain conditions and that Mr Chambers convey to the secretary of the club that their request was granted very reluctantly.' The conditions were almost certainly 'no smoking, no dancing and an 11 p.m. finish' as these were imposed on other youth groups at the chapel. Ten years later the cricket club was still organizing concerts, and in October 1889 permission for use of the large school room was granted without conditions. Had the young people perhaps become more trustworthy?

Everton's growing strength

The 1879–80 season was a good one for Everton and it is an indication of the club's growing strength that it was admitted to membership of the newly formed Lancashire Football Association before the start of the 1880–81 season. That season marked Everton's debut in a cup competition – the Lancashire Cup. As friendlies were the staple diet of football until the introduction of the Football League in 1888, cup games offered spectators the greatest form of excitement. But Everton supporters did not get too much cheer from the first-round tie against Great Lever. After a promising 1–1 draw away from home, Everton were humiliated 8–1 in the replay at Stanley Park. However, the season was redeemed by excellent performances in friendly matches. Of the 17 played, 15 were victories, one was a draw and there was only one defeat. Remarkably, in 11 games Everton's opponents failed to score.

The arrival of 'King John'

Before the start of the 1881–82 season the club appointed its first president, John Houlding, the Liverpool brewer whose house overlooked Stanley Park. After a humble start in working life as an errand boy in a customs house followed by a period as a cowman's assistant, Houlding became foreman in a brewery before going on to set up his own prosperous brewery producing Houlding's Sparkling Ales. An ambitious man, Houlding became a prominent figure in local politics. He was chairman of the Everton Conservative Association and in 1884 he was elected to the city council representing the Everton and Kirkdale ward. He was made an alderman in 1895 and he became Mayor of Liverpool in 1897. He was such a powerful personality that the press nicknamed him 'King John of Everton'. He was to leave a lasting impression at both Everton and Liverpool football clubs.

New colours and the move to Priory Road

There was another change before the start of that season. The club was still playing in a mixture of colours and it was felt that the time had come for a common strip. However, it was considered too expensive to buy a set of new shirts, so when one of the players came up with the ingenious solution of dyeing all the old ones black and wearing a scarlet sash across them as a contrast, the idea was eagerly seized upon. This earned the team the nickname 'The Black Watch' after the famous Royal Highland Regiment of that name. Other colour combinations were later tried until the famous royal blue shirts and white shorts made their appearance in 1901–02.

The 1881–82 season, Houlding's first as president, was a good one. Fifteen out of 20 friendly matches were won while the club went one stage further than the previous year in the Lancashire Cup. Interest in Everton was beginning to grow and on occasions the team was watched by up to 2,000 spectators. But these gates generated no income. The pitch was not enclosed so it was impossible to charge an entrance fee. This was not a situation that Houlding liked.

The impetus to find a new home came as a result of the decision of the parks committee not to allow Everton games to spill over into the cricket season. This prompted Houlding to approach his friend William Cruitt, a wealthy cattle salesman, for permission to rent a field next to his recently built house, Coney Green in Priory Road. It was conveniently near, being just across Stanley Park from where they were already playing. Cruitt agreed to Houlding's request and so, during the summer months of 1883, members of the club worked hard to fence off the pitch and erect a dressing room and a small stand in time for the start of the 1883–84 season.

Twelve months or so before the work at Coney Green began, there was a change of minister at St Domingo's. After five years' dedicated service to the chapel, Ben Chambers, the man who had set the ball rolling in the creation of Everton Football Club, moved with his family to the Southport circuit where he was appointed to be the new superintendent minister. The minutes of the St Domingo Leaders' Meeting of 8 June 1882 pay tribute to his 'faithful and diligent discharge of the duties which have devolved upon him as Superintendent Minister of the Liverpool circuit during the past 5 years' and he was given praise for 'the kind, courteous and impartial manner which he has displayed when presiding over the meetings connected with this church'. Tribute was also paid to his wife, Elizabeth, for the assistance she gave to the church and for 'the kindly influence' she exerted on it.

Chambers' departure represented a great loss to St Domingo's, but he would return at a critical stage in Everton's – and Liverpool's – history.

The 1883–84 season at Priory Road was hugely successful and it was marked by Everton's first trophy win, the Liverpool Cup. The cup campaign started magnificently with the 10–0 annihilation of old rivals St Peter's and after 4–1 and 5–2 successes in the next two rounds, Everton met Earlestown in the final. It was a match that Everton were expected to win easily, having thrashed Earlestown 9–0 the previous week, but it turned out to be a closely contested game with Everton only narrowly squeezing through 1–0. Of the 16 friendly matches played that season, only two were defeats. Everton were making great progress. But the successful season was blighted by the club's eviction from Priory Road. Cruitt had grown tired of the noise and excitement of the supporters and had decided that peace and quiet were more important to him than rent. Everton were asked to leave.

The move to Anfield

Once again it was John Houlding who came to the rescue. He knew that a field off Anfield Road belonging to a friend in the brewery business, Joseph Orrell, had not been put to any use and he believed it would make a good football ground. When he approached Orrell the outcome could not have been more favourable. Orrell concluded a very generous deal with the Everton committee, allowing the use of the field on the following terms: 'That we, the Everton Football Club, keep the existing walls in good repair, pay the taxes, do not cause ourselves to be a nuisance to Mr Orrell and other tenants adjoining, and also pay a small sum as rent, or subscribe a donation each year to the Stanley Hospital in the name of Mr Orrell.' Houlding was appointed the club's representative tenant.

With the negotiations complete, the hard work began. Once again, as at Priory Road, the club members enthusiastically set about the task of transforming the field into a proper ground. The pitch was fenced off, a stand was erected and hoardings were attached to the walls. The finished product may not have looked particularly impressive by modern standards but, unknown to those Everton enthusiasts, they had just made history. Because ironically, they had built the ground that would become famous throughout the world as Anfield, the home of Liverpool FC.

One facility that was not provided at the new Anfield ground was a dressing room. But conveniently, Houlding owned a public house called The Sandon Hotel on the corner of Oakfield Road and Houlding Street just a few minutes' walk from the ground. Here changing facilities were made available for the players. It was a clever move on Houlding's part. It provided him with the perfect opportunity to switch the club's headquarters from the Queen's Head to The Sandon. The move symbolized his growing hold on the club and The Sandon became the focus for all social and official meetings.

The first match played at Anfield was a friendly on 27 September 1884 against Earlestown. Their opponents had no answer to Everton's superior play and were easily brushed aside 5–0. In the next home match two weeks later Everton went one better, thrashing a club from Bolton 6–0. A total of 23 matches were played at Anfield that season, 14 of them victories, two draws and seven defeats. Away form was comparable, with nine wins out of 14 matches and four defeats. The quality of opposition was steadily improving and two recent winners of the FA Cup, Blackburn Olympic and Blackburn Rovers, were among Everton's opponents. Everton again reached the final of the Liverpool Cup and once again they met Earlestown. But this time it was Earlestown who took the trophy after their narrow 1–0 victory.

Before the start of the 1885–86 season Everton decided to turn professional. It was a mark of the club's growing ambition and it ushered in an exciting period of success. The Liverpool Cup was won that season and again the following two. And it was a measure of Everton's progress that when the Football League was created in 1888 for the country's leading professional clubs, they were immediately admitted to membership. Finishing eighth out of 12 in the inaugural season, they were runners-up the next, finishing two points behind Preston North End. But glory was just around the corner. In only the third season of the league's existence – 1890–91 – Everton reached the pinnacle of success by finishing as champions.

George Mahon

One of the leading lights on the Everton committee at this exciting time was George Mahon, senior partner in a Liverpool accountancy firm and one of the most respected men in Liverpool. Although a latecomer to football, he had developed a passion for the game after a friend had taken him to watch Everton play Preston North End in 1887. Two years later, aged 36, he joined the Everton committee. In addition to his love for Everton, Mahon was also a dedicated member of St Domingo's, and was no doubt delighted when the popular Ben Chambers returned as minister in 1890 after an absence of eight years.

In September of that year, only a few weeks after Chambers' return, the chapel's organist resigned. The role of organist was seen to be a key one as the music played in services had a profound effect on the quality of worship. A replacement of the right calibre was essential. But as no one suitable could be found, Chambers turned to Mahon, an accomplished organist, and asked if he would temporarily step into the breach. Mahon agreed but it was not until October 1891, well over a year later, that someone with the desired qualities was found to replace him.

Why did Mahon not offer to take the job on a permanent basis when Chambers first approached him for help? Quite simply, because of acute pressures on his time. The duties of organist were not light and Mahon would have found it too demanding to fulfil them. According to the Minute Book of the trustees' meetings, the requirements were 'to take two services each Sunday and a weekly choir rehearsal and to assist if required in training the scholars for the school anniversary, also to play at any special church gathering'. He already had heavy professional commitments with his accountancy business but, even more significantly, events had been unfolding at Everton that demanded his full concentration and energies . . .

The birth of Liverpool Football Club

The dramatic rise in the club's fortunes and its potential for even further development had caught John Houlding's imagination and his ambition began to drive a wedge between himself and the committee.

As he watched performances improve and attendances grow, he took advantage of his powers as the club's representative tenant to manoeuvre himself into the position of the club's landlord and to change the terms of the tenancy agreement. He began to charge rent in proportion to rise in income rather than at a fixed rate. He also raised the interest on loans he had made to the club.

Not surprisingly, other members of the committee were incensed. They were further appalled when Houlding offered to sell the club land he owned adjacent to the ground at an inflated price. Houlding, for his part, was intensely annoyed when his plans for taking the club forward were rejected. Nor was he pleased by the many teetotallers within the club who were fiercely opposed to the continued use of licensed premises as Everton's headquarters. The relationship with Houlding was breaking down. The crunch came when he confronted the club with a set of proposals and delivered an ultimatum: either accept them or leave Anfield at the end of the season.

But he reckoned without George Mahon. This man was not easily bullied and he faced Houlding square on. It was a battle of the giants. Mahon was an articulate and persuasive speaker, and at a special general meeting attended by 500 members of the club at Liverpool College in Shaw Street on 25 January 1892, he argued so convincingly against Houlding's proposals that all but 18 of those present rejected them. Houlding was bruised. But worse was to come for him: at the club's committee meeting of 15 March he was formally removed from the presidency.

The inevitable happened. With the overwhelming majority of Everton's members against him, Houlding carried out his threat to expel the club from Anfield. He then tried to re-form it on his terms and register it as 'The Everton Football Club and Athletic Ground Company Limited'. But Mahon and the others appealed to the Football Association, claiming that Houlding could not steal Everton's name. The FA Council considered the case and ruled against Houlding in the following terms: 'The Council . . . will not accept any membership of any club bearing a name similar to one affiliated with this Association in the name of the Everton club.' It was a great victory for Mahon and his supporters. But Houlding did not sit back. With four former members of the Everton committee behind him, he was still determined to establish a club at Anfield. The name 'Everton' had been denied him but in the meantime he had thought of another one. And so, in May 1892, he duly registered 'The Liverpool Association Football Club'.

The move to Goodison Park

Mahon had already begun the search for a new ground for Everton. In January 1892 he had come across a site adjoining Goodison Road in Walton called Mere Green. It was, in the words of the club's official centenary history, little more than 'a howling desert'. However, Mahon could see its potential. He negotiated an option to lease it although he was desperately worried about finding the money needed to transform the wasteland into a stadium. He needn't have been. Most of the capital was raised from shares after forming the club into a limited liability company and the shortfall was generously loaned to the club without interest or security by Mahon's good friend, Dr James Baxter, who had joined the Everton committee at the same time as Mahon. It was a magnanimous gesture on Baxter's part.

Work began on Mere Green in the second week of June 1892 and very quickly the desolate wasteland began to assume the form of a football stadium. Incredibly, the job was finished in time for the start of the 1892–93 season. The impressive new stadium was named Goodison Park, after Goodison Road, and was opened amid great ceremony and festivities on Thursday 27 August 1892 by the president of The Football Association, the renowned Lord Kinnaird. Kinnaird still holds the record of nine FA Cup Final appearances as well as being the longest serving chairman in the FA's history. He was a highly respected Christian whose generosity to charitable causes was legendary.

The celebrations began that day with a 4 p.m. dinner at the Adelphi Hotel in Liverpool presided over by George Mahon, Everton's new chairman. The guests then travelled to Goodison Park where the opening ceremony began at 6 p.m. Afterwards the crowd of some 10,000 was entertained by various sporting competitions involving the Everton players. Also on the programme was a concert by a military band while the climax of the evening was a spectacular firework display. It was certainly a day to remember.

The first match at Goodison Park was a friendly on Thursday 1 September 1892 against Bolton Wanderers with 10,000 spectators in attendance. Appropriately, George Mahon kicked off the match and Everton responded to the occasion with a fine 4–2 win. The next day they met Nottingham Forest in the opening league fixture of the season, 14,000 spectators witnessing a 2–2 draw.

Liverpool's first matches

Meanwhile, across Stanley Park at Anfield, Houlding's Liverpool had got off to a flying start. Their first match was a friendly at Anfield against Rotherham Town from the Midland League, also on Thursday 1 September 1892, and it must have given Houlding great satisfaction to watch the resounding 7–0 win. Remarkably, there was not a single Englishman in the Liverpool side that day. Every player had been recruited from Scotland and it earned Liverpool the nickname 'The team of the Macs'. Despite the massive victory, it must have been a great disappointment to Houlding to see only a handful of spectators inside the ground.

The club's application to join the Football League had been turned down because it had yet to prove itself and so competitive life began in the Lancashire League. Two days after the friendly with Rotherham, Liverpool played their first Lancashire League match against Higher Walton. It was an outstanding 8–0 win but once again the attendance was pitiful, a mere 200 turning up. However, news of Liverpool's goalscoring feats was spreading quickly and when they beat Bury 3–0 at Anfield on 24 September to go top of the league, there were about 4,000 to enjoy the spectacle. There was a distinct feeling that this club was going places.

Everton and St Domingo's: the ongoing link

George Mahon will always be remembered as the man who led Everton from Anfield to Goodison Park and who preserved the Everton name, but he did even more for the club. As chairman from 1892 until his death in 1908 (apart from one very brief break) he set up the club's infrastructure and put it on a sound financial footing. He also guided the committee in 1895 to terminate the lease arrangement on Goodison Park and to buy the ground. There was good progress on the playing side during his chairmanship, the club finishing First Division runners-up four times and winning the FA Cup in

1906 by beating Newcastle United 1–0 in the final at Crystal Palace in front of almost 76,000 spectators.

During the whole time he was chairman of Everton, Mahon was a regular worshipper at St Domingo's. In 1903 the position of organist once again became vacant and although Mahon was not asked to step into the breach this time, he was nevertheless one of two people (the other being Will Cuff) invited to assess the abilities of the candidates who had presented themselves for selection.

Mahon died on 9 December 1908 at the age of 55. Remarkably, in view of the energy he expended as chairman of Everton, as a leading accountant and as a faithful servant of St Domingo's, he had never enjoyed good health. On Saturday 12 December, he was buried at Anfield Cemetery, tragically only a week after his 25-year-old son, Herbert. Among the mourners from the world of football were Will Cuff and Alfred Wade, who were there when it all started at St Domingo's.

Cuff, a former pupil of Liverpool College and a prominent Liverpool solicitor, was too young to have played in Everton's early days as St Domingo's but he did have spells as a player with Mount FC and Walton Breck FC until injury forced him to stop. He was a loyal supporter of George Mahon in the rift with Houlding and he became a shareholder of the club in 1892 when it moved to Goodison Park. A determined man with a commanding presence, but warm and friendly, 27-year-old Cuff was invited to join the Everton board in 1895 and six years later, in 1901, he succeeded Richard Molyneux as secretary.

During his time as secretary Cuff, like Mahon, had the great pleasure of watching Everton win the FA Cup for the first time in 1906 and he also thoroughly enjoyed the 1914–15 season when Everton were champions of the Football League. As Everton secretary, Cuff was described in *The Porcupine* as 'one of those men who gets things done' and who had a 'happy faculty for perfect organization' but he was also a great innovator. During the summer of 1909 he took the team to play exhibition matches in Argentina and two years later he created the Central League for reserve teams, serving as its secretary.

In 1918, due to pressure of work with his law business, Cuff resigned as Everton secretary but three years later, in 1921, he was invited to return to the club as chairman, a position he was to hold until 1938. It was a period in which the club achieved some outstanding successes, starting with the Football League championship in 1927–28. That season will forever be remembered for the feats of one of the greatest names in English football history, whom Cuff had signed for Everton in 1925. The legendary Dixie Dean scored 60 goals (still a record) to secure the championship and, unbelievably, he scored a total of 100 goals in all competitions and friendlies that season. With Dean in their side, Everton enjoyed another championship-winning season in 1931–32 and he captained the team in the 3–0 win in the 1933 FA Cup Final against Manchester City at Wembley. As a point of interest, this was the first FA Cup Final in which players wore numbers on their shirts. It was Cuff's idea.

In October 1936, Cuff made another astute signing who was to become one of England's greatest players. It was Tommy Lawton, a 17-year-old prodigy playing for Burnley. Lawton made a big impact with his 34 goals in the team that won the Football League championship in 1938–39. Cuff insisted that Everton would sign only quality footballers, stating in a newspaper report: 'Throughout its history Everton has been noted for the high quality of its football. It has always been an unwritten but rigid policy of the board, handed down from one generation of directors to another, that only the classical and stylish type of player should be signed. The kick-and-rush type has never appealed to them.'

In 1938 Cuff resigned as chairman of Everton to become chairman of the Football League, but the improvements he made to Goodison Park left a mark for all to see as a symbol of his time in charge; it was the first stadium in England with two-tiered stands on all four sides. He did, however, remain a director of Everton until almost the end of his life. Cuff successfully steered the Football League through the difficult war years and he remained at its helm until his death in 1949 at the age of 80.

Will Cuff, like George Mahon, combined his role as chairman of Everton with loyal service to St Domingo's. In 1894, a year before he became an Everton director, he married 26-year-old Jessie Ford of Mere Lane (now Walton Lane) at the chapel. Their two children, Henry and Hilda, were both baptized at St Domingo's. Cuff had been a member of the choir since a boy and he must have been exceptionally talented, because he was appointed choirmaster in 1891 at the age of only 23.

Cuff resigned as choirmaster in 1898, possibly because of pressures from other sources. However, in 1903 he still had a significant say in the music of the church; as mentioned earlier, he was asked along with Mahon to assess candidates for the position of organist. In May 1899 he joined his father as a trustee of the chapel and in 1903 he was asked to be treasurer. He was also the chapel's official solicitor in certain business transactions. It is particularly appropriate, then, that Cuff should have been Everton's chairman when the club celebrated its fiftieth anniversary at St Domingo Chapel in 1928.

Cuff's wife, Jessie, died in 1948 and this terrible blow caused his own health to decline. He died of acute bronchitis in Parkgate, Wirral, on 6 February 1949. Like George Mahon, he was buried at Anfield Cemetery and such was the esteem in which he was held that the procession to the cemetery was a mile long.

Alfred Wade, a coach-builder like his father, Joseph, was the third ongoing link between Everton and St Domingo's. One of Wade's most treasured possessions was the silver trowel his father had used when laying the foundation stone of the chapel. Wade became an Everton director in 1904 and, after a break, was again co-opted to the board in 1921. He remained a director until his death 15 years later in 1936 at the age of 78. During this period he shared with Will Cuff the pleasures of the 1927–28 and 1931–32 championship seasons and the joy of winning the FA Cup in 1933.

Everton and Liverpool reconciled

Houlding's Liverpool won the Lancashire League championship in the club's first season after the split with Everton. They were immediately elected to the Second Division of the Football League and won it at the first attempt, gaining promotion to the top flight. But life in the First Division proved to be much tougher than expected and the team finished the season bottom of the table. Undaunted, they fought back to win the Second Division title the next season and immediately regained their lost status. Something of Houlding's grit and determination was obviously showing through. A promising fifth position was achieved in 1896–97 followed by the runners-up spot the next year. The pinnacle was reached in 1900–01 when Liverpool won the Football League championship. It was to be the first of many.

But John Houlding, the controversial father of the club, did not live to see any more. At the turn of the century he began to suffer ill health and his condition progressively deteriorated. In 1902 he travelled to the warm climate of the south of France to convalesce but it was too late. He died at his hotel in Nice on Monday 17 March aged 69. His body was brought back to Liverpool and his funeral took place on Friday 21 March at the church of St Simon and St Jude near his home. He was buried in Everton Cemetery. In an amazing gesture of forgiveness and reconciliation between the clubs, Houlding's coffin was carried by three Everton and three Liverpool players and flags at both Goodison Park and Anfield were flown at half-mast.

It was a gesture that undoubtedly would have delighted Ben Chambers, whose initiative in starting a cricket team at St Domingo's had been the first step in the creation of these two great clubs. Unfortunately he had died, aged 56, less than four months previously on 28 November 1901 in Leeds. He had been serving there since leaving St Domingo's for a second time in 1894. He was buried three days later in Shepley where he and his wife had grown up.

Sadly, St Domingo's, where everything began, is no more. After celebrating its centenary in 1971 it merged the following year with another chapel to form Oakfield Methodist Church in Anfield. Its site was sold and the building was demolished to be replaced by an old people's residential home. St Domingo's may have gone, but it has certainly not been forgotten. A glance around the Everton club shop confirms that it lives on in the affections of many of the club's supporters and is remembered by them with gratitude.

6

Fulham

When Henry Shrimpton, one of Fulham FC's early players, wrote his history of the club in 1950 he claimed that two clerics were its founders. In fact it was only one. Yet Shrimpton can be excused his faulty recollection. St Andrew's Church, where the club was founded, was a magnet for sports-minded clergymen and no fewer than eight had some involvement with the club in its first 20 years. With such a strong clerical presence at the club it is easy to understand why someone writing 70 years or so after the event should confuse the respective contributions of one or more of them.

The founder of the club

The actual clergyman to whom credit for the foundation of Fulham Football Club is due is the Reverend John Henry Cardwell, who was born at Nunnery Farm, Sheffield, on 20 June 1842. While Cardwell was still a boy his father, William, decided to give up the farming life and move his family to Burnley in order to run a coal merchant's business. The young Cardwell attended Burnley Grammar School and then continued his studies at Caius College, Cambridge. He graduated in 1864 and decided to enter the Anglican ministry. After ordination in 1865 he took up an appointment as curate at St James's Church in Clerkenwell, London, where he served for six years. But it was his move in 1871 to St Andrew's Church in Fulham Fields that will particularly interest supporters of Fulham FC: his appointment as curate there signalled the first step in the creation of their renowned football club.

When St Andrew's was opened in 1868 as a mission church in the large parish of All Saints, Fulham, it served a rural area covered in market gardens. The district had changed little when Cardwell took up his appointment as curate, but within a decade rows of terraced housing had sprung up to accommodate the huge influx of labourers who came to find employment on the railway and other industries in west London. In fact, so rapid was the increase in population that Fulham Fields was created a separate parish in 1874 and St Andrew's was elevated to the status of parish church. Cardwell was appointed its first vicar that same year.

It was a daunting task to serve a parish whose population was growing at an alarming rate and it was difficult for Cardwell to keep up with the many social problems that began to surface. By 1883 two-thirds of Cardwell's parishioners were classified in the Bishop of London's Visitation Records as belonging to 'the labouring poor' and they frequently lived in conditions of overcrowding and squalor. Many of them sought relief from the misery of their existence in alcohol and this in turn led to drunkenness and crime. Cardwell cited drink as one of the major problems in the parish and he worked tirelessly to counter it. He was fortunate to have the loyal support of several members of the congregation who gave dedicated service to the work of the church in this desperately needy parish, and without their help he could not possibly have coped. Two families that stood out for the energetic support they gave him were the Murdochs and the Normans. Those names, together with that of Cardwell, were to go down in history as the pioneers of Fulham Football Club.

The Murdochs and the Normans

The Murdochs were leading figures both at St Andrew's and in the wider Fulham community. Patrick Murdoch was a Scotsman born in 1849 in Kirkpatrick-Fleming, Dumfriesshire, where his father was a church minister. He had come to London to practise medicine and by 1876, at the age of 27, had built up a successful medical practice in Lillie Road, Fulham, among the working-class population of the district. Murdoch was a man of great vision, energy and drive which found expression in church work, politics and sport. He was elected a sidesman of St Andrew's in 1878, a churchwarden in 1879 and became editor of the parish magazine in 1880. His widowed mother, Madeleine, who joined him in London, was also an energetic worker at the church and was particularly active in Sunday School work.

In politics Murdoch was a staunch Conservative and he founded the Fulham Conservative Club in 1884. It was largely due to his efforts that W. Hayes Fisher won the Fulham seat at the ensuing general election. As a sports enthusiast Murdoch directed his energies mainly towards cricket and football but he also enjoyed shooting and fishing. In June 1879, with the help of the Reverend Hyde Edwardes Walker, curate of St Andrew's, he formed the West Kensington Cricket Club and he later became president of Walham Green Cricket Club. However, it was as patron of the football club founded at St Andrew's that he was to leave his mark in history.

The first mention of the Norman family is in the February 1876 edition of the parish magazine, in which Edward Norman is listed as one of the people from whom the magazine was obtainable. Norman, a master house painter, lived at 1 Pownall Road with his wife, Lucy, and their nine children. Lucy was a teacher at the infants' Sunday School in Star Lane (now Greyhound Road) and in addition to her teaching responsibilities she organized many children's parties there. The Sunday Schools were booming at St Andrew's during the 1870s and 1880s and the need for more teachers became desperate. Members of the Norman family stepped in to help. In October 1879, 17-year-old Clark was assisting his mother and a month later his 21-year-old sister Nora joined them. By 1885 their brother Tom (then 21) had also been recruited.

The Revd Cardwell took a great interest in work with young people and numerous organizations were set up at the church for them. He wanted the young to feel welcome, stressing this in the parish magazine of June 1876: 'We are convinced that many are alienated from the Church by being driven from its doors when they are young, and we are most anxious that this should not be the case in this large and rapidly expanding parish.' Cardwell did much to improve the quality of the lives of the young people in the parish. In addition to organizations for them within the church, free hot dinners were provided for the poorest children of the neighbourhood and thanks to willing helpers such as Lucy Norman, as many as 160 children at any one time could take advantage of these meals.

The formation of the club

But despite all this, Cardwell felt that more should be done for the youths of the church. He had often seen Tom Norman and his friends enjoying cricket and football and as a firm believer in 'recreation and good fellowship', according to his book *Twenty Years in Soho*, he was convinced that sport was the answer. With this in mind he approached Tom Norman sometime in 1879 with a proposal. There is no record of the actual words of their conversation but there can be little doubt what they discussed: the formation of a cricket and football club at St Andrew's. Cardwell must have been delighted with Norman's response to his idea. The 15-year-old enthusiastically set about the task of recruiting players and before the year was out the St Andrew's Cricket and Football Club was up and running.

As the new club's title suggests, cricket initially took precedence over football. At the time, Association football was only 16 years old and it could not compete with cricket as a national pastime. Indeed, it was often no more than a winter activity for cricketers who wanted to keep themselves fit and it would seem that this was how Tom Norman and his friends viewed the game. It perhaps also explains why the reports Norman submitted to the parish magazine contain accounts of the club's cricketing activities but make no mention of football. Similarly, the local press in Fulham began to report cricket matches in 1874 but did not consider football matches newsworthy until 1881, and then only in the briefest form.

The club that Tom Norman formed seems to have been little more than a youth club with a sporting emphasis during the first four years of its existence, and it is unlikely that Cardwell ever intended it to be much more than that. If, to quote from the parish magazine, the club brought 'benefit and blessing to themselves and the neighbourhood' he would have been well satisfied. But he did not leave the youngsters entirely to their own devices. As one of the patrons of the club (the other was Dr Patrick Murdoch) he took an active interest in their activities and gave them support and encouragement. No doubt, too, they received encouragement from two curates at St Andrew's, both cricket enthusiasts, the Revd Walker and the Revd Rowland Cardwell, the vicar's younger brother.

In the very early days from 1879 to 1883, the members of the club probably only played for fun among themselves. Kit was informal: the footballers simply turned out in whatever rough clothes they could find. Some wore long trousers, others wore shorts, some played in old-fashioned knickerbockers. A few wore caps. Footwear consisted of old leather boots with bars of leather nailed across the soles and heels to prevent slipping. As changing rooms were non-existent the players simply changed at home.

The club's first football 'ground' was an area of unenclosed rough land adjoining the Sunday School in Star Lane where Tom Norman's mother taught. It was hardly suitable for a football pitch. The playing area was so small compared with standard size pitches that the school wall had to serve as one of the goals. Furthermore, the surface was of such poor quality that the pitch became known locally as the 'Mud Pond'. A ground such as this is unlikely to have tempted many teams to savour its delights, so any friendlies that may have taken place against other clubs would probably have been played away.

It was not until 1883 that there was a significant change of direction at the club. The members were now in their very late teens and they were beginning to take the game much more seriously. By the summer of 1883 they felt the time had come to abandon the hopelessly inadequate 'Mud Pond' and find a proper pitch. They must have been delighted to be offered one at the Ranelagh Club (a country club for wealthy gentlemen) close to the Putney Bridge railway arch. As the Ranelagh Club had no dressing rooms, changing facilities were provided at the nearby Eight Bells public house in Fulham High Street. Everything was now in place for the start of the 1883–84 season and, significantly, this was the first season in which the club's cricket and football results appeared in the local press and reports of the activities of the cricket section appeared in the parish magazine.

The first match reports

Although a St Andrew's team was first mentioned in the *West London Observer* of 12 November 1881, it is fairly certain that the team that lost 4–0 to Grove House that day was from the church of that name in Shepherd's Bush where the match was played. At the time there were a number of football teams in London called St Andrew's, but as early match reports gave no team line-ups and only occasionally mentioned the goalscorers it is often impossible to identify which team is which. Before 1886, when Norman's club changed its name to Fulham St Andrew's Cricket and Football Club to avoid confusion, a certain amount of detective work by historians is necessary to establish who is who.

It was not until Saturday 25 August 1883 that a report appeared in the *West London Observer* mentioning recognizable names from St Andrew's, Fulham. But the report was of a cricket match, not a football match. It took place on Saturday 18 August 1883 at Baron's Court where St Andrew's met another church team, St Matthew's. (The pitch on which this game was played was on the site now occupied by the prestigious Queen's Club of tennis fame.)

Later that year, on 13 October, the *West London Observer* contained a report of the football match between St Andrew's and Stanley at Eel Brook Common in Fulham which Stanley won 4–2. This was almost certainly the first of the many local derbies between the two clubs and although no St Andrew's players were named, it can reasonably be assumed that this was the first reference in the local press to the St Andrew's, Fulham, football team.

On Saturday 25 November 1883 a 'very pleasant game', according to the *West London Observer*, took place at Willesden Junction between Christ Church Rangers and St Andrew's. St Andrew's played the match a man short and Rangers made the most of their advantage by winning the game comfortably 4–0. When the two teams met again the following season at the same venue, St Andrew's gained their revenge when captain Jack Howland scored the only goal of the game. No one could possibly have guessed that these two clubs would one day meet again under names that would be instantly recognized throughout the world of football. In 1886, just three years after the defeat to Tom Norman's side, Christ Church Rangers merged with St Jude's Institute to form the renowned Queen's Park Rangers Football Club.

It was not until 28 February 1885 that a football report appeared in the local press with a full St Andrew's line-up for a 2–0 win against Beaumont. The team was listed as: Read (goal); W. Hobson and Smith (backs); King, Johns and Hobson (half-backs); Norman, Johnson, Howland, Freds and Stone (forwards). Three of these players – Jack Howland, Jack King and Tom Norman – had been members of the club from its earliest days in 1879. They were regulars in both the football and cricket teams but they were also loyal members of the St Andrew's Sunday School. In fact, all three of them would in time become teachers there, Howland eventually attaining the position of assistant superintendent.

Tom Norman

Tom Norman, of course, was the one who had formed St Andrew's Cricket and Football Club at Cardwell's suggestion. He was its first secretary and was responsible for arranging matches and sending reports of the club's activities to the parish magazine and the local press. Born Thomas Robert Norman in Ipswich on 1 December 1863, he was the youngest of four children, three boys and a girl, but before he was three years old his family had moved to Fulham where three further sisters and a brother were born. After leaving school he trained to be a carpenter but eventually he became a master builder.

Norman was married on 11 August 1891 to Mary Jane Rowe and no doubt a few eyebrows were raised on their wedding day because of the considerable age difference between the couple: Norman was 28, his bride was a 40-year-old widow. It would also have surprised many, in view of the Norman family's commitment to the Church of England, that the wedding took place at St Thomas's, a local Roman Catholic church. Perhaps Norman's marriage was the beginning of a drift away from St Andrew's, because only four years later he ceased to play for the club he had formed.

The arrival of Peregrine Propert

The St Andrew's club had always enjoyed the full support and patronage of the vicar, John Cardwell, but in May 1885 an addition was made to the clergy staff that was to give added status to sport at the church. That month a former Cambridge Blue and one of the top oarsmen of his generation, the Reverend Peregrine Propert, came to assist at St Augustine's in Lillie Road, a mission church attached to St Andrew's. Propert was a colossus in the rowing world, renowned for the many prestigious competitions he had won. His profile in the sport was further heightened when he helped found the National Amateur Rowing Association.

But it was not just as an oarsman that Propert had gained a reputation. He was also renowned as an exceptionally strong swimmer. As a 17-year-old in 1879 he became the first person to swim across Ramsey Sound, the treacherous mile-wide strait with many dangerous cross-currents and rapids off the coast of Pembrokeshire in

South Wales. This remarkable feat was not to be repeated for another 56 years despite numerous attempts to do so. Never one to shirk danger, at the same age Propert became a member of a lifeboat crew near St David's where he grew up. He was also a fearless cliff climber and his sporting talents extended to cricket and football.

It is hardly surprising that this exceptional sportsman should almost immediately associate himself with the St Andrew's Cricket and Football Club on his arrival at the church. As he was only 23 he was no more than two or three years older than most of the St Andrew's players and this, combined with a shared love of sport, would have drawn him to them. They, in their turn, would have been keen to get to know him as his reputation as a sportsman is bound to have preceded his arrival.

Propert was born on 20 October 1861 in Haverfordwest, Pembrokeshire and grew up in nearby St David's where his father was a highly respected barrister. He entered Trinity Hall in the University of Cambridge in 1881 and very quickly established a reputation as an oarsman. He was made captain of the college boating club and his team of eight became the best in the university. In addition to his rowing talents, Propert also represented Trinity Hall at football. An outgoing person who mixed easily with others, he enjoyed an active social life at university, and among other things he helped to form the Footlights amateur dramatic society.

Propert had entered Cambridge with fairly clear career plans in mind but while there his thinking was turned upside down. In an article in the *Fulham Observer* of 31 May 1935, he explains what happened:

> My earliest intention was to take up law and politics, but fortunately at Cambridge I met a group of men who, although the leading athletes at the university, were also men of deep religious convictions. My association with them changed my outlook upon life. I felt there was something better to aim at than worldly success, and that was the service of God and my fellow men.

The group who made such an impact on Propert have become known in history as 'The Cambridge Seven'. These devout Christian men, all from very privileged backgrounds, caused a sensation throughout Britain when they announced in 1885 that they were giving up fame and fortune to become missionaries in China. So remarkable was the news at the time that it commanded as much public interest as the plight of General Gordon in Khartoum.

Four of the seven were student contemporaries of Propert at Cambridge. The most famous of them was Charles Thomas (C. T.) Studd, a cricket superstar of the day. He was captain of Cambridge University and also an England regular. But at the very height of his fame, 24-year-old Studd gave up the game to become a missionary. In January 1884 he had attended a meeting in St Pancras to hear the renowned American evangelist Dwight L. Moody and as a result his life was transformed: 'Formerly I had as much love for cricket as any man could have, but when the Lord Jesus came into my heart, I found that I had something infinitely better than cricket.' From that time on he wanted nothing less than to share 'the joy of my salvation' with the entire world and he started with his friends. He persuaded several members of the England cricket team to hear Moody speak and as a result four of them became Christians.

Propert was deeply challenged by the change in Studd's life and by the profound impression that two more of the Cambridge Seven had made on him. One was Stanley Smith, the stroke oar of the Cambridge boat, the other was Arthur Polhill-Turner, a former member of the Eton cricket eleven and, like Propert, a member of the Trinity Hall football team. Both had become Christians after attending Moody's evangelistic meetings in Cambridge in November 1882 and both were as enthusiastic as Studd in sharing their faith with others. As a result of his association with these three men Propert left Cambridge a convinced Christian determined to serve God and his fellows. As he explained in the *Fulham Gazette* of 25 January 1935, more than anything else he wanted to 'take up work in some poor and crowded district'.

He did not know where or how to begin but out of the blue in May 1885, a year or so after his graduation, some relatives in West Kensington informed him that there was a vacancy at St Andrew's Church in Fulham not far from where they lived. By coincidence Propert was due to go up to London from St David's that month to row for the Henley Rowing Club and while in London he decided to visit Fulham. He found what he was looking for: '[I] made up my mind that here there was work for me to do . . . I felt that there was something more than mere bricks and mortar in Fulham.'

After an interview with John Cardwell a few days later, Propert was invited to assist at St Augustine's Mission, which had been opened by St Andrew's in February. Although Propert was not yet ordained, Cardwell was quite prepared to engage him in view of the urgent need for extra staff to cope with the demands of a parish whose population was growing at the rate of 3,000 per year. St Augustine's Mission, according to a leaflet it produced appealing for funds, stood at the centre of a population of over 6,000 'consisting chiefly of mechanics, railway servants, labourers, costermongers [fruit sellers], those engaged in laundry work, and the abjectly wretched' and they were served by a single clergyman, the Reverend Arthur Brittain. He needed help and Propert's arrival was timely.

Having started at St Augustine's, Propert never looked back and he was to serve there faithfully until his death on 18 February 1940 at the age of 78. Propert was a man of the people and he took every opportunity he could to establish close practical relationships with the inhabitants of the district. This included the use of sport as a vehicle for outreach to young people. Shortly after his arrival, a gymnasium was opened at the mission and he wasted no time in putting it to good use. He had previously met some youths who worked in a nearby cabyard and he felt that the new gym would offer them a safe and moral environment in which to unwind and make new friends. He knew that these youths were looked down on by respectable people as hooligans because of their foul language, unkempt appearance and lack of education and he was also fully aware that his association with them would be regarded in many quarters with contempt. But he dismissed such considerations as irrelevant. His congenial manner, genuine concern for their welfare and prowess as a sportsman soon earned their affection and respect. His own account of those days, as told to the *Fulham Chronicle* of 31 May 1935, is revealing:

> among them I worked and made some of my best friends, some of whom remain [so] to this day. On Saturday nights we had very simple sing-songs, and some came to our services on Sundays. We had a gymnasium, and boxing became very popular; in this I took a very prominent part, and from this little place we turned out a national, as well as international champion. At this time I was rowing for the Thames Rowing Club first eight, and when I brought home silver trophies and cups it produced great excitement and admiration. My association with these young fellows, whose language was not always

classical, produced much criticism from the 'respectable', some of whom went so far as to say I was not fit to be a clergyman, and reported me to the Bishop, Dr Temple . . . I explained [to Dr Temple] that I had come not merely to preach but to apply Christian principles as far as I could in Lillie-road. I believe I convinced the good Bishop that my critics did not really understand the gospel message 'I came not to call the righteous but sinners to repentance.' I think even now the church has largely forgotten this truth. We are terribly respectable.

The visits to Crowborough

When Propert became involved with the St Andrew's Cricket and Football Club, it was already well established; in fact the football section was running a second eleven. Much of the credit for the club's growth is due to Dr Murdoch, who was a guiding light on the committee. His steadying influence and financial support had helped create a structure which not only established the club as a credible organization but also laid the foundations upon which its future success was built.

The influence of John Cardwell, too, was significant. Some indication of his commitment to the club can be seen from his generous gesture in inviting the entire cricket team in August 1885, wholly at his own expense, to spend a short holiday at his country residence in Crowborough in Sussex and play a match against the local team. The match ended in defeat for St Andrew's but a year later the club had an opportunity to gain their revenge when Cardwell repeated his generous gesture.

One of the additions to the side for the 1886 visit was Propert. The Crowborough band was in attendance for the occasion but it was St Andrew's who called the tune that day, winning the match decisively by an innings and four runs. Propert's inclusion had certainly helped make a difference. He played for the team on more than one occasion and while he may not have been a regular – no doubt other responsibilities took up too much of his time – he continued his involvement with the club and its players, especially the footballers, for many years. When Jack Howland died at the age of 44 in 1909, it was Propert who conducted his funeral service at St Augustine's. Some indication of the lasting impression Propert made on the footballers is evident from the fact that Henry Shrimpton, in his 1950 history of

Fulham FC, actually named him, along with Cardwell, as one of the club's founders!

Changes of name and the first trophy

With men of the quality of Cardwell, Murdoch and Propert behind the club, it made rapid progress. The 1886–87 football season was a particularly memorable one. First, there was a slight change of name. The confusion with other teams called St Andrew's had become unacceptable and it was decided to start the season with 'Fulham' in the club's title, the full name now being Fulham St Andrew's Cricket and Football Club. Secondly, it was the club's most successful season to date. Of 22 games played, 21 were won but the outstanding achievement was without doubt winning the West London Association Cup, the club's first trophy. This was secured after a 2–1 victory in the final against another church team, St Matthew's.

The semi-final of that same competition was reached the following year but there were to be no further trophies until 1891 when the newly inaugurated West London Observer Challenge Cup was won. In the interim, however, there were two important developments. The first was the growth in the club's popularity that made it possible to field a third eleven in the 1887–88 season. The second was another change of name. In January 1889 the momentous decision was taken to simplify the club's title by shortening it to 'Fulham Football Club'. There is no evidence to suggest that this in any way represented a break with St Andrew's Church. There was no marked change in personnel as Tom Norman and Jack King, two of the founders, were still in the side and Dr Murdoch remained active on the committee. Nevertheless, the nickname 'The Saints' disappeared in the local press from this date and cricket ceased to be a part of the club's activities.

The first enclosed ground

After spells at a variety of grounds the club secured its first enclosed pitch in the summer of 1891 at the Half Moon ground behind the boathouses in Putney. (It was shared with the Wasps Rugby Club.) By this time the public was beginning to take a real interest in the club and on occasions attendances reached almost a thousand. As it was now possible to charge threepence admission, these gates represented a considerable boost to the coffers.

Another big stride forward was taken in 1892–93 when Fulham entered two cup competitions for the first time, the London Senior and the Middlesex Senior Cup, and also became members of the newly formed West London League. Although no cups were won that season, the team stormed through the league, winning 16 of its 18 matches and drawing the other two to take the championship in convincing style. Founder member Jack King and his brother Will were regulars in the side, and it must have given Jack great satisfaction to see how far the club had progressed since its early days at the 'Mud Pond'.

More clergymen at the club

An important newcomer to the team that season was the Reverend Gilbert Hall, who had been appointed curate of St John's Church, Walham Green, not long before the season started. Hall was an outstanding defender and as a student at St John's College, Oxford, had won a football Blue for representing the university. He made a significant contribution to the championship success as he was part of a very strong defence that conceded only eight goals. He played again the following season but it was to be his last, probably because church commitments took up too much of his time. However, as he attended the 1896 annual dinner he clearly did not lose touch with the club.

But Hall was not to be the last clergyman to be involved with the club. For the second time in its history a clerical presence was established at the top when the vicar of All Saints, Fulham, the Reverend William Carter Muriel, was appointed president in succession to Cardwell. (Cardwell had left Fulham to become rector of St Anne's, Soho, in 1890.) Muriel, vicar of All Saints from 1890 until his death in 1916, was club president until 1898, the year it turned professional. He served the club faithfully during his presidency and regularly attended its major social functions.

The move to Craven Cottage

Although Fulham Football Club was developing at a rapid pace, the link with its past remained strong, at least until the arrival of professionalism in 1898. Tom Norman was making the occasional appearance until 1893–94 and Jack King was still in the team a season later. Dr Murdoch meanwhile continued to play an important part in the club's affairs, for instance persuading his good friend Hayes Fisher, the MP for Fulham, to become a patron in 1895.

Despite the club's progress, it could never aspire to really great things until it had a permanent home of its own. A major breakthrough occurred in 1894 when a derelict site with potential for development as a football ground was found on the north bank of the Thames. A cottage belonging to Lord Craven had been built on the site in about 1780 but it was destroyed by a fire in 1888 and the land had become a wilderness. In its day Craven Cottage, as the building was known, had seen many distinguished visitors including the Prince of Wales (later Edward VII), Emperor Napoleon III of France and the Prime Minister Disraeli.

The club acquired the site but it was to take two years of hard work and determination to turn it into a football ground. For one thing it was six feet below river level and had to be raised to the appropriate height. This was imaginatively achieved using material excavated from the new Shepherd's Bush underground railway station. As another good example of recycling, the borough council donated road sweepings which were used for the creation of embankments. The hard work was finally rewarded when, on 10 October 1896, the club's first senior match was staged at Craven Cottage. Appropriately enough, this historic occasion was marked by a comfortable 4–0 win for Fulham against Minerva in the Middlesex Senior Cup.

In the 1896–97 season, the first at Craven Cottage, Fulham entered the FA Cup for the first time and also joined the London League. The following season, with two Nonconformist ministers in the side (the club was obviously still a magnet for clergymen!), the championship of the London League was won without a single defeat. Ambitions were riding high and 1898–99 saw the arrival both of professionalism and entry to the Second Division of the Southern League, the best in England outside the Football League. Four years later, in 1903, the club entered a new phase of its development when it became a limited company with the official title 'The Fulham Football and Athletic Co. Ltd.'

The upward rise continued: promotion to the First Division of the Southern League in 1903, two successive league championships in

1906 and 1907 and admission to the Second Division of the prestigious Football League in the 1907–08 season all followed. And in time the club that had started with a group of youthful enthusiasts in the unlikely setting of a cramped, muddy piece of wasteland would join the élite of English football in the FA Premier League. How amazed Cardwell, Murdoch and Norman would have been to see their little church club in such illustrious company. But now that their part in the story of the club's rise to greatness has been told, surely the concluding chapters of their own stories deserve some mention.

Cardwell, Norman and Murdoch: the final chapters

Cardwell, the prime mover in the club's creation, remained at St Andrew's until December 1890 when, at the age of 48, he left Fulham for St Anne's in Soho. St Anne's was a very difficult parish in the heart of London rife with prostitution, drunkenness and violence and Dr Temple, the Bishop of London, left Cardwell under no illusions when he invited him to accept the position: 'You are still in your prime and well able to undertake a second difficult task.'

Cardwell's book *Twenty Years in Soho* gives a fascinating account of his experiences at St Anne's. Almost immediately after his arrival he invited his parishioners to a social gathering in order to introduce himself to them. As at St Andrew's, the social dimension of church life was a feature of Cardwell's ministry at St Anne's. He firmly believed that it was 'the way of relieving the dullness and monotony of many lives by providing the brightness and good fellowship which is too often only found in the public house'. It was also his conviction that people's hearts were won not 'by an aggressive propaganda' but by a policy of 'making friends first and converts afterwards'. As at St Andrew's, he was mindful of the needs of the young. When the new St Anne's parish hall was built he did not miss the opportunity of fitting a gymnasium in the basement for their use.

Despite the obvious strains of working in such a demanding parish Cardwell maintained a sense of humour. He found it particularly amusing, for instance, that a little girl he knew persisted in calling him 'Mr Cardboard'. His other fond memories of St Anne's included the presence of Queen Alexandra at the church to attend the Passion service and the invitation to the choir to sing in the chapel of

Buckingham Palace before the Queen and her sister, the Empress of Russia.

Cardwell remained at St Anne's until his retirement in 1914. He died seven years later in Ealing on 17 April 1921 at the age of 78. His obituary in the *Church Times* paid the following tribute to him: 'Though ever a fighter for truth and right, he had the gift of being able to fight without bitterness and without losing friends. No priest in the London Diocese was more universally beloved.'

Tom Norman's last known appearances for Fulham were two London Senior Cup ties against Caledonians in October 1893. At the start of the 1894–95 season, aged 30, he left the club to join Hammersmith Athletic. After that there is no trace of him. He does not appear in the 1901 census nor can any record of his death be found. Did he perhaps emigrate?

Dr Patrick Murdoch retired from his medical practice in Fulham and returned to his native Dumfriesshire in the late 1890s. He became a prominent member of the Dumfriesshire County Council and remained an active worker for the Conservative Party until his death on 21 August 1912 at the age of 63. He almost certainly kept in touch with his old friend Hayes Fisher in Fulham, from whom he would have heard about developments at Fulham Football Club.

These three men feature only briefly in histories of Fulham FC but the debt the club owes them is incalculable. The vision of Cardwell, the drive and energy of Murdoch and the youthful enthusiasm of Tom Norman all played a crucial part in setting the club on its way to becoming one of the foremost in England. They found neither fame nor fortune through football; the pleasure of 'recreation and good fellowship' was reward enough for them. Fulham supporters have every reason to recall the names of these illustrious pioneers of their club with pride.

7

Manchester City

❖

Of all the famous football clubs founded by churches, only one can claim to owe its origin to the initiative of a woman. That unique distinction belongs to Manchester City. It was a remarkable young woman, Anna Connell, a clergyman's daughter, who took the first important step that was to lead to the creation of one of the great football clubs of England. When she started a Working Men's Meeting at St Mark's Church, West Gorton, in 1879 out of concern for the rough, tough types who lived there at the time, she could hardly have guessed that her charitable action was to have lasting repercussions for the world of football.

The Connells arrive at St Mark's

Anna Connell was born on 24 December 1851 in Clones, County Monaghan, Ireland. She was the daughter of Arthur Connell, a clergyman, who, like Anna, was destined to play a significant part in the story of Manchester City Football Club. Arthur trained for the Anglican ministry at St Aidan's Theological College in Birkenhead and was ordained deacon in 1856. He was to serve the Church of England for 40 years, during which time he won the deep affection and respect of the parishioners to whom he ministered.

Connell's first appointments as curate were in County Down in the north of Ireland, first in Lurgan then in Tullylish. So highly was he regarded in Tullylish that when he was offered the curacy of Christ Church, Harrogate, in 1859, the congregation tried to persuade him to stay by offering him a stipend equivalent to the one he would receive at Christ Church. But it was to no avail as Connell clearly felt called to Harrogate. He duly left for England with his wife Anna and his two daughters, Anna and Georgina, to embark on a ministry that was to last almost seven years and which, according to his obituary in

The Gorton Reporter, was 'much blessed and greatly appreciated'. He developed such a bond with the congregation there that he once declined a remunerative position with the British and Foreign Bible Society in response to a heartfelt plea for him to stay. But eventually, after almost seven years in Harrogate, Connell moved on. In 1865 he received and accepted the invitation to become the rector of the newly built St Mark's Church in West Gorton, Manchester. It was an appointment that was to have huge significance – it signalled the beginning of the history of Manchester City Football Club.

On Saturday 13 April 1864 the foundation stone of the new St Mark's Church had been laid. About a year and a half later, on Thursday 30 November 1865, the church was consecrated. The following Tuesday Arthur Connell was inducted as the first rector. At the time of his induction, his eldest daughter Anna was just 13 years old. Little did he know what an impact she was to have in the parish when she was an adult.

Social conditions in West Gorton

When Arthur Connell came to West Gorton, it was still a small semi-rural town but it would rapidly be swallowed up by neighbouring Manchester, then in the midst of an industrial boom. During the course of his 32 years' ministry at St Mark's – he retired in 1897 at the age of 75 – the composition of his parish was to change dramatically. In fact, it would not be long before the social problems that beset Manchester would arrive on his own doorstep.

By the 1850s Manchester had become the victim of its own success. It was one of the world's largest manufacturing centres, and as 'The Queen of the Cotton Cities', to quote Angus Reach in the *Morning Chronicle* in 1849, it had attracted, and continued to attract, thousands of workers from rural communities in England leaving poorly paid agricultural occupations in search of higher wages. They were joined by thousands more newcomers from Ireland and continental Europe, all eager for a better life with a higher standard of living. However, the reality was to be quite different. As there was no ready accommodation for this tidal wave of new arrivals, it had to be found quickly, easily and, above all, cheaply. The solution was the construction of row upon row of back-to-back terraced houses that mushroomed in the rapidly disappearing countryside around Manchester.

But quantity was not accompanied by quality. Terraced houses were built in vast numbers from the 1840s right up to the 1890s, but no consideration was ever given to the wellbeing of the occupants. Living conditions were invariably cramped and squalid, and in some areas there were on average only two toilets for every 250 people. Furthermore, earnings were too low to make possible any means of escape to more desirable districts. A graphic description of the appalling environment in which thousands of people lived is painted in a letter by Archibald Prentice to *The Manchester Times* on 20 July 1844: 'The houses . . . are cluttered together with more regard for the saving of ground-rent than for the comfort and health of their in-habitants. In many districts the crowding of houses into narrow, dark, ill-drained and ill-ventilated alleys and lanes, and the cramming of persons into these miserable dwellings is frightful to contemplate.'

By the 1880s Manchester's urban sprawl, with all its attendant social problems, had reached West Gorton, which was now virtually indistinct from its giant neighbour. In 1890 West Gorton's separate identity disappeared altogether when it was officially incorporated into Manchester. When Sylvia Pankhurst, daughter of the famous suf-fragette leader Emmeline Pankhurst, arrived with her father in the area on his campaign trail on behalf of the Independent Labour Party in the 1890s, she saw sights not unlike those described by Archibald Prentice in *The Manchester Times* some 50 years earlier:

> Often I went on Sunday mornings with my father to the dingy streets of Gorton . . . and other working-class districts . . . Those endless rows of smoke-begrimed little houses, with never a tree or flower in sight, how bitterly their ugliness smote me! . . . I would ask myself whether it could be just that I should live in Victoria Park, and go well fed and warmly clad, whilst the children of these grey slums were lack-ing the very necessities of life. The misery of the poor . . . awoke in me a maddening sense of impotence; and there were moments when I had an impulse to dash my head against the dreary walls of those squalid streets.

It was the inhabitants of those squalid streets that formed the nucleus of the parish that Arthur Connell was called to serve. Such was the poverty in the area that in the late 1870s a soup kitchen was opened in the immediate neighbourhood of St Mark's Church, and in the words of *The Gorton Reporter* of 4 January 1879, 'crowds of poor, famished-looking creatures pressed to that place, where soup and bread were provided in order to satisfy the cravings of nature'. But it wasn't just poverty that afflicted the inhabitants of West Gorton. There were other huge social problems – one of which was drink.

The main place of escape for working men from the drudgery of their mind-numbing daily work, and from the cold, cramped hovels in which they lived, was the public house. And by the late 1870s there were plenty of them in West Gorton, offering warmth, good company, and the good cheer of alcohol. But was it really good cheer? Not in the light of the frequent acts of drink-induced violence recorded in *The Gorton Reporter*, or the pitiful sight of hungry and shoddily clad children whose fathers had squandered the family's entire food and clothing allowance on ale. When the Union Iron Works, the largest local employer with a workforce of 700, celebrated its twenty-first anniversary at a special dinner on Saturday 11 September 1880, the proprietor, Mr S. Brooks, felt it necessary to say to those assembled: 'I would also point out to you the benefit of using your spare time and holiday times in a rational way; not in wasting your energies and robbing your wives and families by drinking.' Although drink may have been a form of escape from one set of troubles, it was certainly the cause of many more.

It wasn't only drink that was a menace in West Gorton. Throughout the 1870s and into the 1880s street warfare had become a favourite pastime of local young men who enjoyed a pitched battle with invading gangs from other areas. This particular form of 'recreation' was known locally as 'scuttling', and young men would often participate in these fights in frighteningly large numbers. On Saturday 3 May 1879, for instance, *The Gorton Reporter* gave an account of a battle that had taken place during the week in West Gorton's neighbouring district of Bradford-cum-Beswick, stating that more than 500 had taken part in it. Nothing was done to put a stop to these disturbances as residents who lived close by were too frightened to inform the police for fear of their windows being smashed in retaliation. It seemed that the gangs were in control and that the streets of West Gorton and its neighbouring districts would never be trouble free.

Anna Connell establishes the Working Men's Meetings

It was in 1879 at St Mark's Church that a positive step was taken to address these problems. Anna Connell, the rector's eldest daughter, now a young woman of 27, decided something had to be done. She was grieved by the wretched existence of the men of the parish and the aimlessness of their lives, and wanted to help. But how could she get them out of the pubs and off the streets? What alternative could be offered to them? Then she remembered that two years previously her younger sister Georgina – at the age of only 23 – had started regular Mothers' Meetings at the church. Their purpose was to give the women of the parish the opportunity to meet together in a relaxed environment where they could hear spiritually uplifting talks and enjoy a programme of wholesome leisure activities. The first meeting was held in the church vestry but it did not seem to be a very promising start – only seven women attended. But then the numbers grew so steadily that only a year later – in 1878 – a parish hall had to be built at the corner of Hyde Road and Ashmore Street which was capable of accommodating 100 people. Such was the popularity of the meetings that even this became inadequate to meet the demand. It was Anna's conviction that something similar for the men of the parish would prove to be an attractive alternative to the pubs and the streets.

Certain that this was the answer, and with her father's full support, Anna resolved to set up a weekly Working Men's Meeting offering a programme of spiritually edifying talks and wholesome entertainment consisting of musical evenings, concerts, singing, drama, readings and recitations – typical forms of amusement at a time when there were no cinemas, TVs, radios, DVDs, CDs or other kinds of electronic entertainment.

With the idea fully formed in her mind, Anna felt that the recently built parish hall would be the ideal venue for the men's meetings. This was duly made available for Tuesday evenings. Anna then embarked on house-to-house visits to inform the men of the parish about the meetings, and to invite them to attend. On completion of her house calls, she no doubt looked forward to the first meeting with some excitement, expecting that the men would arrive in large numbers to enjoy the programme on offer to them. But she was to be disappointed – the very first Tuesday only three men turned up. It probably crossed her mind that only two years previously a working men's club in the locality, which had provided a programme of lectures on subjects of interest and at which alcohol and gambling were banned, had failed through lack of support. Was this to be the fate of her meetings, too? What should she do now? Should she abandon the scheme as a failure? Or should she persevere, believing that the club could succeed despite all the signs to the contrary?

To the eternal gratitude of generations of Manchester City supporters, Anna Connell did not throw in the towel. This plucky young woman was not a quitter. Despite the massive setback she had just experienced, her resolve to help the men of the parish did not weaken in the slightest. She was also greatly encouraged by the full backing and support she received from two stalwarts of the church – 44-year-old William Beastow, a sidesman at St Mark's, and 37-year-old Thomas Goodbehere, one of the churchwardens. These men were well known in the locality, not only as leading members of the church but also as senior officials of the Union Iron Works, just a stone's throw from St Mark's. They were strategically placed, therefore, to spread the word to the large workforce at the iron works about the Working Men's Meetings. Moreover, Beastow had been president of the working men's club that had failed two years previously in the district and he no doubt drew on his experience to advise Anna about potential pitfalls to avoid in the formation and running of her own group.

Anna's dedication and persistence eventually won the day. After a disastrous start the membership of the Working Men's Meetings grew to over 100 with an average weekly attendance of around 65. Remarkably, only a few months after she had taken the first step in forming this new association, the men wanted to show their appreciation. At a tea party held on Tuesday 6 January 1880 *The Gorton Reporter* records that they made Anna a presentation 'in acknowledgment of her valuable service in presiding at their meetings'. By 1882, according to a later report, the meetings had become so well established that Captain Anstruther, the Archdeacon of Manchester, told the men at one of their Saturday evening sessions that 'it must be a great source of encouragement to see how the movement had been taken up, and the highest credit was due to Miss Connell for the way in which it had been carried out. No man could have done it – it required a woman's tact and skill to make it so successful.' And it continued to be successful. When Anna left the parish in 1897 to look after her father in his retirement, the Men's Meetings were still going strong. Indeed, a variant of them continued at least until the 1960s, possibly even until 1974 when, sadly, the church was demolished.

The purpose of the meetings was to help the men develop their faith and to find encouragement for living the Christian life. From time to time talks were given by visiting speakers about Christians whose lives were an inspiration to everyone. The men responded well to the talks and Arthur Connell was obviously delighted with the group's progress. In March 1882 the local press reported that he was very pleased 'with the intelligent interest' the working men took in their meetings. Later that year Captain Anstruther remarked, according to *The Gorton Reporter* of 13 May 1882, that 'none could believe the amount of good the meetings had done.'

The birth of St Mark's (West Gorton) Football Club

Fired by Anna Connell's vision and enthusiasm, William Beastow threw himself wholeheartedly into the development of the new group, not only chairing many of the Tuesday evening meetings but also thinking of ways in which the growing bond between the men could be further strengthened. Then, in the late spring of 1879, he had an idea that was to have historic consequences. With summer rapidly approaching, he was aware that the thoughts of a great number of sporting enthusiasts throughout England would be turning towards a favourite seasonal pastime – cricket. He quickly recognized that this popular sport could be used to attract more members to the men's meetings, and he therefore proposed the formation of a working men's cricket team, with players being recruited from among those who attended Anna Connell's Tuesday meetings. The idea met with an enthusiastic response and a squad was easily recruited in time for the start of the cricket season.

The team obviously enjoyed their first season because they were playing together again in the summer of 1880. In fact, such was the spirit of camaraderie that developed among them that they decided to form a football team in order to continue their sporting activities together during the winter months. And so, in the winter of 1880 in St Mark's parish hall a new football club with the name 'St Mark's (West Gorton)' was born. The Reverend Arthur Connell, ever supportive of worthwhile initiatives in the church, agreed to be its president, William Beastow was appointed chairman, and Frederick Hopkinson became the secretary. It was to be the start of something big.

The first matches and grounds

No club records exist of the matches played during 1880–81, its first season, but reports of seven games appeared in the local press. It is possible, however, that others were also played. The first known St Mark's match took place on 13 November 1880 on an area of rough ground believed to have been next to the Union Iron Works in Thomas Street, a street running parallel to Clowes Street where the church was situated. Their opponents that day were Macclesfield Baptist Church. Although 11-a-side had been established as the norm by the FA in 1870, there were no official restrictions on the numbers of players that could appear in a side in friendly matches. It was nothing out of the ordinary, therefore, when these two church teams agreed before the match to play 12-a-side. The 12 who represented St Mark's were: W. Sumner (capt.), Walter Chew, J. Collinge, W. Downing, H. Heggs, Frederick Hopkinson, Richard Hopkinson (the organist at St Mark's Church), Edward Kitchen, A. McDonald, J. Pilkington, and the chairman's two sons, Charles and John Beastow. Unfortunately for St Mark's, the Baptists proved to be the stronger side in that historic encounter, winning the match 2–1. In fact, St Mark's were to record only one victory in the 1880–81 season, a 3–1 away win against Stalybridge Clarence on 19 March 1881. And it was not a particularly glorious victory. Only eight of the home side turned up, and three volunteers from the crowd had to be recruited at the last minute to make up the Stalybridge numbers.

The following season St Mark's switched their home venue to the Kirkmanshulme Cricket Club on Redgate Lane, close to the Belle Vue Zoological Gardens. The ground there offered a playing surface far superior to that of the rough land adjoining the Union Iron Works. It was not a particularly inspiring season but it is memorable for one match that was to have huge significance in the history of football. It was the 3–0 away defeat to Newton Heath on 12 November 1881. Nobody could possibly have foreseen that this was the first derby match between two clubs that would later take the football world by storm. They would become better known as Manchester City and Manchester United . . .

The stay at the cricket ground proved to be a short one. The cricketers, horrified by the state of their pitch which had cut up very badly by the end of the 1881–82 season, decided that the footballers had to go. St Mark's had no option but to search for another ground. They eventually found one less than a mile from the church at Clemington Park, just off Queen's Road. However, events surrounding this move are unclear. It seems that the ground was shared with another local side, Gorton Athletic, and that there was some degree of merger from 1882 to 1884 between the two clubs. It is not known if Arthur Connell continued as president during this period, nor, indeed, who was actually responsible for the running of the club.

Change of name to Gorton AFC

The merger, whatever form it took, was neither harmonious nor long lasting. For one reason or another, considerable friction had been developing between members of the two clubs and this eventually peaked in the summer of 1884. At that point two of the St Mark's contingent, Walter Chew and Edward Kitchen, decided they had had enough and walked out. In October they set up a new club and called it Gorton Association Football Club. Chew and Kitchen had been members of the original St Mark's team, and they were soon joined by others who had been involved with that club. William Beastow once again took up his position as chairman while Kitchen became secretary. The link with St Mark's Church was further consolidated when another churchwarden, James Moores, a director of the Union Iron Works, was appointed president. This new Gorton club was to go from strength to strength while the Gorton Athletic club left behind at Queen's Road, after a brief spell under the name of West Gorton Athletic, eventually disappeared altogether.

Gorton AFC's first important task was to find a suitable ground. Fortunately Lawrence Furniss, a young forward at the club, came across a piece of rough ground off Pink Bank Lane near Belle Vue station, not far from the Kirkmanshulme cricket ground. He suggested it would serve the club's purposes well. The committee agreed and the site was secured. This was not to be the last time that Furniss would play a significant part in the club's history. He was destined to become one of its most influential figures during the course of the next fifty years, serving as secretary, chairman, director and president. He was also closely involved with St Mark's Church for many years, eventually becoming a sidesman.

The committee was determined that the club should be properly organized and at about this time applied for membership of the Manchester & District FA. The application was successful. Beastow, the chairman, was also keen that the team should have a recognizable identity on the pitch, and so, to this end, he personally provided the club with a set of black jerseys with a large white cross. The cross was not simply decoration; it symbolized the club's roots as a church team. Beastow, a churchwarden of St Mark's, wanted this fact formally and visibly acknowledged.

The strong and continuing link with St Mark's Church is evident from the report of Gorton AFC's first annual dinner that appeared in *The Gorton Reporter* at the end of the 1884–85 season. Almost all the names mentioned were recognizable as members of the very first St Mark's team or committee. Fred Hopkinson read the Annual Report, which was positive in every respect except the quality of the ground.

The need for a good ground was obviously a major concern, and there must have been a frantic search for one during the summer of 1885 in time for the start of the new season. A suitable area of land owned by the Bull's Head Hotel on Reddish Lane was eventually found. It was about three miles from St Mark's Church, the furthest the club had been away from the place of its birth. It was available for an annual rent of £6, which included use of the pitch plus changing facilities at the hotel. But this was not to be a permanent home. At the end of the second season there, the landlord increased the rent to an unaffordable level, forcing the club to search for its sixth home in only seven years of existence.

It was club captain K. McKenzie, a Scot, who found the next ground. It was an area of very rough land off Hyde Road belonging to the Manchester, Sheffield and Lincolnshire Railway Company. Once convinced of the potential of this land, the committee decided to negotiate rental terms with its owners, and gave Walter Chew and Lawrence Furniss the task of leading the negotiations. For a club in search of a permanent home the agreement they reached of seven months' rental for a total of £10 may have seemed very short term, but it was a start. They could discuss extensions later.

Another change of name – Ardwick AFC

With the land secured, the hard work began. By the end of August 1887 the bumpy wasteland had been transformed into an enclosed football ground with an acceptable playing surface. All was now ready for the start of the 1887–88 season. All, that is, apart from a new name for the club. Having relocated from the Gorton district, it was felt that its current title was no longer appropriate and so the decision was taken to adopt the name of the district to which the club had moved – Ardwick. On 23 August 1887, Gorton AFC officially became Ardwick AFC. New headquarters were found at the Hyde Road Hotel, only a short walk from the ground, where changing facilities were provided for the players on matchdays and a room made available for committee meetings. Both the hotel and the ground were to remain the focus of the club's activities for 36 years until the move to Maine Road in 1923. Obviously the deal that Chew and Furniss had struck with the railway company for the use of the land off Hyde Road was not as short term as it looked!

In one sense the move to Hyde Road was something of a home-coming for the club as the ground was only a third of a mile from St Mark's Church, its birthplace. But the geographical proximity to the church was not accompanied by any closer spiritual affinity with it. In fact, the club was most definitely losing the link with its church roots. Significantly, there was a change in the presidency. James Moores, senior churchwarden at St Mark's, stepped down as president and Stephen Chesters-Thompson, a brewer, was invited to replace him. The link with Chesters' Brewery was to be a strong one lasting some 30 years, and it was not long before the club acquired the nickname 'The Brewerymen'. This is hugely ironic when it is remembered that one of the reasons why Anna Connell formed the Working Men's Meeting at St Mark's was to get the men of West Gorton out of the pubs.

The move to professionalism

Chesters-Thompson was an ambitious man and he wanted to develop the club as a serious business concern. It was not long before he was joined on the committee by another wealthy backer, John Allison, who had made his fortune developing various forms of pain relief with water treatment at his hydro in Hyde Road in Ardwick. With the financial support of these two wealthy businessmen the club was now able to raise its sights. The first priority was to find players of proven quality and between May and October 1890 Allison and Lawrence Furniss (now secretary) recruited seven professionals from Bolton Wanderers and a further five from Scottish clubs. At the same time as improving the playing squad, a considerable amount was also spent on ground improvements.

With the professionals on board, performances on the field reached new heights. In October 1890 Ardwick entered the FA Cup for the first time and thrashed their opponents Liverpool Stanley 12–0 in the first qualifying round at Hyde Road. However, for some unexplained reason the club did not take up its place in the next round. The mysterious exit from the FA Cup was quickly forgotten a few months later when, on 18 April 1891, Ardwick beat local rivals Newton Heath 1–0 to gain their first trophy, the Manchester Cup. Fired by this success, the committee decided that, after 11 years of friendlies and occasional cup ties, it was time to join an organized league. And so, at the start of the 1891–92 season, the club became a member of the Football Alliance, a league just one level below the Football League, the best in the land. It was a propitious move because the very next season the Alliance was absorbed into the prestigious Football League, forming its Second Division.

The final change of name – Manchester City

But then things started to go drastically wrong. By October 1893, as a result of dreadful mismanagement of its finances and poor results on the pitch, Ardwick AFC was in crisis. With plummeting attendances and an ever-growing queue of creditors it looked as if the club would have to fold. The committee therefore took the decision to play out the remainder of the season and then call it a day. However, a colourful character called Joshua Parlby, the licensee of the Wellington Hotel on Stockport Road who had recently replaced Lawrence Furniss as club secretary, used his gifts of persuasion to convince members of the committee and a large number of season ticket holders that the club still had a future, but only if it made a fresh start as a limited company under a new name. He insisted that the name chosen should be one with which the whole of Manchester could identify, and he therefore duly proposed 'Manchester City Football Club'. The proposal was accepted.

On Monday 16 April 1894, Manchester City Football Club Limited officially became a registered company and shortly afterwards it was accepted into membership of the Second Division of the Football League in place of its forerunner Ardwick AFC. The future was now assured. And what a glorious future it was to be – eight FA Cup Final appearances (four as winners), three Football League Cup Final appearances (two as winners), two Football League championships (the top flight at the time), and winners of the European Cup Winners' Cup. Who could possibly have foreseen that Anna Connell's Working Men's Meetings at St Mark's Church would one day lead to all this?

Arthur and Anna Connell: the final chapter

But what became of Anna herself, and of her father the Revd Arthur Connell, the first president of St Mark's (West Gorton) FC? As Anna never married, she continued to support her father in his ministry at St Mark's until July 1897 when he was forced to retire on health grounds. By this time she and Arthur were the only members of the Connell family still at St Mark's, Georgina having married in September 1889 and Arthur's wife, Anna senior, having died in March 1895.

Arthur Connell had been suffering for two years from paralysis of a vocal cord and chronic bronchitis, and when it became obvious that he could no longer continue, he felt compelled to resign from the rectorship. The news was received with great sadness in the parish. A measure of the great respect in which he was held, and the affection that was felt for him, can be gauged from the warmth of the speeches made at his farewell presentation on Saturday 17 July 1897. As reported in *The Gorton Reporter*, one speaker stated that the rector was 'loved and admired for his faithfulness and steadfastness' and several others expressed the wish that he would stay despite his infirmities. They argued: 'A man teaches by what he is, and the sight of Mr Connell walking through the streets would have reminded the people that his life and example was one they could follow.' But Connell's doctor made it perfectly clear that this was out of the question, stating 'that the Rev. Arthur Connell is not in a fit state of health and strength to perform the onerous duties which devolve upon him as rector of St Mark's, West Gorton, nor is there any hope that he will ever again be equal to such a burden'.

By this time Connell's voice had failed completely, and he was unable to speak to his parishioners at the presentation. Instead, his daughter Georgina's husband, the Reverend John Dixon, read aloud the farewell address that Connell had written. In it Arthur clearly stated what was the bedrock of his faith: 'I trust my preaching has been of no "uncertain sound". Christ, and Him crucified, was the theme on which I delighted to dwell, knowing there was no subject more saving in its power and sanctifying in its influence.'

Arthur Connell had served his parish well. During his 32 years at St Mark's he had set up, or supported, numerous organizations for the wellbeing of his parishioners. He had also created the climate and conditions that made it possible for a football club to be born there. Significantly, there were thriving football and cricket clubs at the church at the time of his retirement. But his most spectacular success was the development of schools for the local children. These included day schools for boys and girls, a Sunday School and, for the very poor, a Sunday Evening Ragged School. All these schools experienced a phenomenal rise in attendance during the course of his ministry. At the Ragged School alone there were 850 children in attendance by the time he left. *The Gorton Reporter* of 3 July 1897 commented: 'These schools, together with the bright, hearty and evangelical services of the church have contributed to the mental, moral, social and religious elevation of the whole district, and many are now occupying responsible and remunerative positions in Manchester and elsewhere whose success in life has been largely due to their connection with St Mark's.'

It was not overlooked at Arthur Connell's farewell presentation that Anna, too, had played a significant part in the work of the church. A presentation was made to her also, and warm words were spoken in praise of her. It was stated that 'Miss Connell had been a devoted daughter to their esteemed rector, and by her aid he had been able to carry on much work that would have been left undone without her aid.' Particular appreciation was expressed for her work for the men of the parish: 'Miss Connell had been a mother to the fathers in their neighbourhood. Miss Connell organised a men's meeting at which they gathered weekly, and there she came to speak words of comfort and encouragement to them . . . this part of Miss Connell's work had been fully blessed as many men in their parish could testify.'

The Connell family had worked as a very close team in the ministry at St Mark's. All of them had played a very significant part. Anna and Georgina, in addition to their work with the working men and mothers of the parish, also helped out at entertainment events by playing the piano, singing, or giving readings and recitations. The Archdeacon of Manchester once commented that Arthur Connell was the father of the parish, his wife Anna was the mother of the parish, and his two daughters Anna and Georgina were the curates. When it is remembered that Arthur Connell did not have the services of a curate until August 1883 – 18 years after his appointment as rector – the importance of the support of his family can be fully appreciated.

In July 1897 Arthur, accompanied by Anna, moved to the seaside resort of Southport to live in retirement at 17 Marshside Road. It was hoped that the clean air of the town would help alleviate his severe bronchial problems. He did enjoy another 18 months of life, but, on Friday 24 February 1899 at the age of 77, he finally succumbed to bronchitis. So great had been the affection and respect for him at St Mark's that arrangements were immediately made to transport his coffin from Southport to Victoria Station, Manchester, from where it would be met by a horse-drawn hearse and conveyed to St Mark's for his funeral service. This took place on Tuesday 28 February. The church was packed. Among those attending were William Beastow and Thomas Goodbehere, who had helped Anna set up the Working Men's Meetings, and two former players from the football club's early days, John Beastow and Lawrence Furniss. After the service the cortège proceeded to St James's, Birch, where Arthur was buried with his wife.

His eldest daughter, Anna, was now living alone in Southport. It was only natural, then, that Georgina should invite her to come and join her family in Walsall where her husband, John, was the vicar of St Paul's Church. Anna readily accepted the invitation.

Three years later, Anna made an emotional return to West Gorton with Georgina on 25 April 1902 for their last known public appearance there. As the parish magazine records, it was for the unveiling of a memorial tablet at St Mark's in memory of their father. Anna unveiled the tablet at the end of Evensong with the dedicatory words

'I unveil this tablet to the honour and glory of God, and in memory of my father, in the name of God the Father, Son, and Holy Ghost.' The tablet was erected on the south wall of the church 'as an expression of esteem and affection by Parishioners and Friends'.

Anna was to remain with Georgina and John for the rest of her life, living first at St Paul's vicarage for 14 years and then moving with them to Darlaston rectory in Walsall when John was appointed rector of Darlaston in 1913. The rectory was her home for the next 12 years, but sadly, towards the end of her life, she suffered from heart problems and died there on 21 October 1924 at the age of 72.

Anna had spent the last 26 years of her life in Walsall, and she was no doubt happy there, living in the company of close family members. But it is with Manchester that her name will always be associated because of the Working Men's Meetings she had started in 1879 that led to the creation of Manchester City FC. Supporters of this great football club have every reason, therefore, to remember the name of Anna Connell with gratitude.

8

Queen's Park Rangers

————•◦•————

The story of Queen's Park Rangers Football Club actually begins when a new housing estate of striking architectural interest was built during the 1870s and 1880s in the Kensal Green area of west London. This remarkable estate of 'cheerful, healthy and properly constructed homes for the industrial classes', as it was described by a director of the company that built it, was named 'Queen's Park' in honour of Queen Victoria. In the same year that the estate was completed – 1886 – some of its youthful residents decided to name their new football club after it. This humble little club was to become one of the best known in England.

The Queen's Park Estate

What was so remarkable about the estate that inspired the name of a famous football club? Like Bournville village in Birmingham and Port Sunlight village in Merseyside, it was created by enlightened individuals who aimed to provide decent housing in pleasant sur-roundings for working-class people. In 1867 the Artizans', Labourers' and General Dwellings Company Limited (ALGDCL) was set up by William Austin to provide proper housing for workers after his own experiences as a labourer had made him painfully aware of the appalling conditions of squalor and overcrowding that low wage earners were forced to live in. Although Austin left the company in 1870, his ideals lived on and in 1873 the ALGDCL completed its first 'workman's city' in London, the Shaftesbury Park Estate. That same year it began work on a second such 'city', the Queen's Park Estate.

The plan was to build houses for 16,000 people on an 80-acre site with a road layout of six parallel avenues numbered 'First' to 'Sixth', criss-crossed by roads lettered from A to P. But much more than housing was envisaged. Four of the 80 acres would be turned into a garden and recreation area, all the streets would be lined with plane trees and there would be shops, a coal depot, a dairy farm, baths, washhouses and a lecture hall. It was reported in *The Times* of 16 September 1874 that 'every opportunity will be taken to promote and develop temperance principles' and so 'reading rooms, discussion clubs, libraries and other substitutes for the public house' would be provided. In fact, so great was the emphasis on an alcohol-free environment that no public houses were permitted on the estate and no shops were permitted to sell alcohol. Any residents found drunk were evicted. The estate had a high moral tone. *Artizans and Avenues*, a 1990 history of the estate, quotes the company's policy that only 'the most quiet and provident portion of the industrial classes' were permitted to live there. This was the very respectable environment in which most of the first Queen's Park Rangers players grew up.

The club's first headquarters

The moral tone of the area was reinforced by the parish church, St Jude's, which was situated just beyond the eastern perimeter of the estate in Lancefield Street. St Jude's was to play a very prominent part in the foundation of Queen's Park Rangers. The church officially opened its doors as a place of worship on Saturday 13 August 1878 but by 1882 the population of the estate had grown so much that the vicar of St Jude's, the Reverend Sidney Bott, decided to establish a St Jude's presence in the heart of the estate itself. He therefore bought a site on the corner of Ilbert Street and Fourth Avenue in order to build a mission hall there. The hall was opened two years later, in 1884, as St Jude's Institute. This was to become the headquarters of Queen's Park Rangers until 1898.

The Boys' Brigade at St Jude's Institute

Sidney Bott, the first vicar of St Jude's, had great vision and energy and he served the parish faithfully for 34 years until his retirement in 1912 at the age of 65, three years before his death. His achievements as vicar were considerable, particularly in the ongoing fight against alcohol abuse, but it is has not been recognized that he also made a significant contribution to the history of Queen's Park Rangers. The key to this was the support and encouragement he gave to young people in the parish.

One of the young people's activities he encouraged was the Boys' Brigade. As an organization, the Boys' Brigade had been founded on 4 October 1883 in Glasgow by William Alexander Smith, whose stated objective was 'the advancement of Christ's Kingdom among Boys, and the promotion of habits of Obedience, Reverence, Discipline, Self-respect and all that tends towards a true Christian manliness'. Smith was a Sunday School teacher who believed that good discipline was fundamental to good Bible teaching. He felt that the two could be more effectively combined through a semi-military format that involved, among other things, the wearing of a uniform and engaging in physical activities such as drill, athletics and camping. Bands were also a prominent feature. Smith's idea quickly caught on and the success of his own company of 30 boys led to the rapid spread of Boys' Brigade companies throughout Britain. Membership requirements were that boys had to be between the ages of 8 and 19 and that each company should be connected with a church or other Christian organization. The vicar or minister usually held the rank of chaplain. By 1885 a company of the Boys' Brigade had been established at St Jude's Church, using St Jude's Institute as its meeting place.

The club's founders

One of the members of the Boys' Brigade at St Jude's was John ('Jack') McDonald, a key figure in the foundation of Queen's Park Rangers Football Club. McDonald was born in Glasgow in 1869 but as a young boy he left Scotland for London with his widowed mother, Christine, his brothers William and James, and his sister Elizabeth. Jack was the youngest of the children by several years. Their father, Robert, was a carpenter. Jack did not follow in his father's footsteps but became a clerk. The family settled on the Queen's Park Estate, their first home being 32 C Street. The streets of the estate at the time were simply named as letters of the alphabet but in January 1884 surnames of people, mostly connected with the ALGDCL, were added to the letters. (Thus 'C Street' became 'Caird Street'.) The McDonalds subsequently moved to 2 Enbrook Street. This was Jack's home when, at the age of 24, he married 20-year-old Ellen Hutchings, a local girl from the estate, on 25 October 1893 at St Jude's.

On his arrival from Glasgow, Jack McDonald became a pupil at D (later Droop) Street Board School, now Queen's Park Primary

School. Opened in 1877, it was the first school to be built on the estate and it was here that McDonald developed the passion for football that he was never to lose. The spacious school playground provided the arena for McDonald and his football-loving schoolmates to hone their emerging skills each playtime. Their enthusiasm for the game was no doubt also carried over into their leisure hours, to any open space they could find near their homes. These youngsters, mostly in their early teens, were quite content to enjoy impromptu games arranged among themselves but by the time they had reached their mid-teens they were ready for something better. A big step was taken sometime in 1885 when, in a discussion with the others, McDonald and his friend Fred Weller proposed the formation of a football club.

Fred Weller, like Jack McDonald, was not a native Londoner. He was born in 1867 in Wallingford, Berkshire, where his father, James, worked as a carpenter. Fred also trained to be a carpenter. After working in Wallingford for a while, he decided to look for better opportunities in London. Fred came to the Queen's Park Estate where he found lodgings at 114 Ilbert Street with David Birrell, a railway porter, and his family. It turned out to be a good choice of accommodation because he met his future wife there, marrying Birrell's eldest daughter, Mary, in 1892. But he also met Jack McDonald soon after his arrival on the estate and their friendship was to have great significance in the history of Queen's Park Rangers.

The birth of the club

Weller and McDonald had probably got to know each other at St Jude's Institute where numerous activities were provided for young people. The Boys' Brigade was one of them and McDonald and Weller had both become members, along with several of McDonald's old class-mates from Droop Street School. All the boys shared a great love of football and McDonald and Weller took the lead in arranging impromptu games between themselves. When in 1885 the two proposed the formation of a club, the idea was warmly received by the others.

Agreement was quickly reached that the new club should be named after the place where they frequently met – St Jude's Institute.

They would, of course, first need the approval of Sidney Bott, the vicar, before they could form a club with the name of the church in its title. But Bott was so enthusiastic about the idea that he not only allowed the boys to use the Institute as their club's official headquarters but also set up a gymnasium for them there. Had Bott withheld his support at this crucial time, there would have been no Queen's Park Rangers.

The members of the new St Jude's Institute FC agreed to pay a subscription of seven shillings and sixpence (37½p) for the season to provide money for essential club purchases. In the beginning the only equipment they possessed was four upright posts and two pieces of tape to string between the posts as they could not afford crossbars. These items were stored at the Institute and carried to the field they used as a pitch.

The first games

St Jude's Institute Football Club duly got under way at the beginning of the 1885–86 season but it is not known who their first opponents were. The earliest reported match was an away game on Saturday 20 February 1886 at Roundwood Park, Willesden, against Vulcan FC third eleven, the result being a 4–0 win for the Vulcans. Unfortunately there are no details of the team line-up in the *Willesden Chronicle* match report. Only the result and the venue are stated. Association football was not taken very seriously by the local press at the time, rugby being the only winter sport that really mattered. However, it is known from other sources who some of the earliest players were. In addition to Jack McDonald and Fred Weller, the founders, they included Henry ('Harry') Creber, Tom Handford, Albert Pearsall and the brothers Henry ('Harry') and Joe Spurr. Remarkably, there were considerable age differences between these players. At the start of the season Albert Pearsall was only 12, Joe Spurr was 14 while Harry Spurr was 20. McDonald and Weller were 16 and 18 respectively.

The merger with Christ Church Rangers

Details of other St Jude's games have proved to be very elusive but one match in particular has gone down in the history of Queen's Park

Rangers, even though the result and team line-ups are not known. It was against Christ Church Rangers in the spring of 1886. The two sides knew each other well as most of the players lived on the Queen's Park Estate. Christ Church Rangers had been formed in 1882 from a boys' club started by the Christ Church Mission in Ponsard Road on the College Park Estate. This estate was virtually the same age as Queen's Park but it did not enjoy the benefits of its near neighbour as housing was of much poorer quality and the physical environment was nowhere near so attractive. It is not known how the youngsters from the Queen's Park Estate became involved with the mission in College Park. Perhaps they had friends who went there?

After the match against St Jude's, one of the founder members of Christ Church Rangers, George Wodehouse, was on his way home when a friend who had come to watch him play suggested a merger between the two sides. He felt that a combined team would be much stronger than either team could be separately. This idea was put to both clubs for consideration. The point was taken and a merger was agreed. But when the newly combined team played under the name of St Jude's Institute and used the Institute as its headquarters many of the Christ Church players claimed that they had been victims of a takeover and they walked out angrily. Their response was to set up a rival club called Paddington FC. St Jude's and Paddington would later meet . . .

A new name and the arrival of Charles Young

It was important that the few remaining members of Christ Church Rangers should feel fully included in the union and to achieve this a new name acceptable to everyone had to be found. It was E. D. Robertson who came up with the perfect compromise. He suggested that as almost all the players lived on the Queen's Park Estate, the name of the estate should be incorporated into the club's title and that it should be coupled with the word 'Rangers' to show continuity with the former Christ Church Rangers FC. It was an inspired choice as it did justice to everyone. It was duly adopted.

Just as Sidney Bott had supported the launch of St Jude's Institute FC, so, too, did he show his support for the new Queen's Park Rangers club by allowing St Jude's Institute to be used as its headquarters. But in 1886 another St Jude's clergyman, the 25-year-old curate, Charles

Gordon Young, became even more actively involved in the club's affairs and exerted a powerful influence upon it. Young was born in the small Yorkshire village of Oughtibridge near Sheffield on 4 April 1861. His father, Edward, was a brickmaker but he eventually became a successful mining engineer. By 1881 the family had left Yorkshire and was living in Camberwell, Surrey, at which time Charles was working as a clerk to the surveyor of taxes. But he felt called to the Church of England ministry and in 1883 he entered the London College of Divinity to train as a clergyman. Three years later he was ordained and took up his first post as curate, working for Sidney Bott at St Jude's. That year, 1886, was an important one for Young. Not only was he appointed curate of St Jude's but he was also married there on 21 December to Mary Bishop of East Dulwich, daughter of George Bishop, heraldic printer to Queen Victoria.

And the year was equally important for Queen's Park Rangers. Not only had the club chosen the name by which it would always be known, but it also enlisted the services of Young as centre-forward at a crucial point in the club's development. Apart from being a goal-getter, Young was also a leader who was able to fuse the two factions of the club together in a spirit of unity. Having had no previous involvement with either St Jude's Institute FC or Christ Church Rangers, his leadership was seen to be wholly neutral. Young's presence became a stabilizing factor at the club during his two years as curate of St Jude's, both on the pitch and at committee meetings. There is no doubt that his steadying influence helped lay the foundation for success in future years. His departure from St Jude's in 1888 to become rector of Chipstead, near Redhill, in Surrey, must have caused great sadness among the QPR players. They were losing a very good friend indeed.

The early days as Queen's Park Rangers

The question of a suitable pitch was always a major concern in the early days. Christ Church Rangers had played on a field between College Park and Willesden Junction but it was decided that the new Queen's Park Rangers club should play its home games on a piece of land very close to the Kensal Rise Athletic Ground. Money was short at the time and the team must have looked slightly ridiculous in the riding pants they had been loaned by a supporter who owned stables in Maida Vale. However, things began to improve and a short time later a better pitch was secured for a rent of £8 per year at Welford's Fields to the west of Queen's Park, a public park opened in 1887 not far from the estate. Changing facilities were provided in a nearby public house. But in 1889 the club was on the move again, this time to the London Scottish ground in Brondesbury where an entry fee to watch the team play could be charged. However, it was a risk. The rent here was £20 per year and good attendances were essential if they were to cover it. Unfortunately Rangers were not yet the major attraction they were to become and as one game earned gate receipts of only one shilling and sixpence (7^1/2p), the warning signs were clear. Added to this, the pitch had little to commend it. It was constantly waterlogged and at times was in such a bad state that home matches were transferred to opponents' grounds. The club saw no future here and after only a year decided to leave.

There are few records of the games played on those early pitches. The first match report involving Queen's Park Rangers in the *Willesden Chronicle* was an away game to Harlesden United on Saturday 10 November 1888. It was another year before the second Rangers match report appeared in the local press. This time it was the second eleven who were featured but apart from the fact that they defeated Canterbury FC first team 2–1 on Saturday 23 November 1889 at Kensal Green, no match details are given.

After leaving the London Scottish ground in Brondesbury the club became even more nomadic and it is hard to keep up with their many changes of home venue. Sometimes only a handful of games were played at one ground. In fact, when Rangers arrived at Loftus Road in 1917, their present home, it was their sixteenth move. Despite this nomadic existence, the club seemed well organized and Jack McDonald and Fred Weller gave good leadership at committee meetings in the St Jude's Institute. A second team was now well established and a full set of fixtures for both the first and second elevens was completed in the 1890–91 season. It is also evident from results that the club was becoming a force to be reckoned with. The lack of a settled home ground seemed to have little adverse effect in 1890–91 as there were some outstanding successes, including 7–0 against St Bartholomew's Hospital (Fred Weller scored one of the goals), 8–0 against St John's Hammersmith and the 10–0 demolition of Clapham.

The club also entered three cup competitions that season and made good progress in two of them. Rangers' first ever cup match was a second-round tie in the London Senior Cup at home to Tottenham Hotspur in front of a crowd of 500. The result was a 1–1 draw, Jack McDonald scoring for Rangers. The replay was lost 2–1. In the other two competitions, the West London Challenge Cup and the West London Observer Cup, Rangers reached the semi-finals. Although they actually qualified for the final of the West London Challenge Cup after a 4–2 victory against Hanwell in the semi-final (Jack McDonald scored two of the goals), the final for some strange reason did not take place.

Rangers join the West London League

The 1891–92 campaign was a disappointment after the promises of the previous season. The only results of note were 4–1 away wins against Ilford Park and St Albans, Jack McDonald scoring a goal in the latter. But this forgettable year was followed by one that would long be remembered, not entirely for the best reasons. Rangers had secured the use of a pitch at the Kilburn Cricket Club ground on Harvist Road before the season had begun. It was the club's first enclosed ground and the move here seemed to inspire a new level of optimism accompanied by a growing sense of ambition. The club took the bold decision to abandon their staple diet of friendly matches and join the West London League. But they may have regretted it after two league encounters with their bitter rivals Paddington FC, the club formed by the Christ Church Rangers dissidents who had refused to merge with St Jude's.

The first match against Paddington took place on 15 October 1892 at Harvist Road. Rangers wore green and white hoops to avoid a clash with the Paddington strip but this was the only clash they managed to avoid. The Paddington players went into each tackle mercilessly and in scenes more reminiscent of a battlefield than a football match, many of the Rangers team limped off the pitch at the end so badly hurt that they were unable to play for several games afterwards. The result – a 2–0 win for Paddington – was of little consequence in the light of the appalling behaviour of the Paddington players. The return match on 7 January 1893 at Paddington's ground was equally farcical, but for a completely different reason. When they saw the state of the pitch, the Rangers team refused to play but the referee insisted that the game should go ahead. Rangers, however, were resolute and would not step onto the pitch. The referee started the game without them. Paddington kicked off and promptly scored but as there were no opponents to kick off after the goal, the referee abandoned the match and declared Paddington 1–0 winners. These were not happy memories of the first season in league football.

The first trophy

On a much happier note, however, the season was redeemed because Rangers gained their first ever trophy, winning the West London Observer Cup on 22 April 1893. Their opponents in the final at the Kensal Rise Athletic Ground were Fulham, champions of the West London League. In their two league encounters with Fulham, Rangers had managed a 2–2 draw at home but had lost 2–0 away. They started the final as underdogs but rose to the occasion and emerged as 3–2 winners in a closely contested match that went into extra time. It must have been a proud day for keeper Harry Creber, the only known survivor of the St Jude's Institute team of 1885 in the side, to see how far the club had come.

After the successful cup campaign, some of Rangers' best players left to join other clubs. As the remaining squad was not considered strong enough to continue playing in the league, Rangers withdrew from it and reverted to friendlies as their staple diet. Three years later, however, the team had been strengthened sufficiently for the club to take the ambitious step of entering the FA Cup competition for the first time. They were drawn at home against Old St Stephen's in the first qualifying round and the match attracted a club record crowd of 3,000. The result was a 1–1 draw but Rangers lost the replay 1–0 and progressed no further.

The record gate for the cup match inspired the club to move to a bigger ground, and where better than the venue of their first great triumph, the Kensal Rise Athletic Ground? With a ten-year lease on the site, the club was now in a position to join the Second Division of the London League for the start of the 1896–97 season and provide more attractive opposition for its growing army of supporters. It proved to be a wise decision because Rangers gained promotion. However, the club decided to withdraw from the First Division after only four matches in 1897–98 and revert to friendlies, probably because it was felt that prestigious friendlies against some of the country's top clubs were a more attractive proposition than league encounters with less challenging local sides. Some very famous clubs came to Kensal Rise that season, including Everton, West Bromwich Albion and Woolwich Arsenal. High attendances justified the decision to leave the league, 6,000 spectators, for instance, turning up to watch the Arsenal game.

The move to professionalism

The club was clearly becoming more ambitious and its ambitions were reinforced by success in three rounds of the FA Cup in 1897–98. The next logical step was to turn professional. The decision to do so was taken in consequence of an FA Cup preliminary round match against Richmond Association on 24 September 1898. But it was not because of a confidence-inspiring result. In fact, Rangers lost the match 3–0. It was the consequences of an incident that occurred during the match that propelled the move towards professionalism. Sammy Brooks, one of the Rangers players, had been sent off for foul play, for which the London FA fined the club £4 and closed its ground for 14 days. Rangers considered this punishment to be unduly harsh and they promptly withdrew from all London FA competitions in protest. But in doing so they merely shot themselves in the foot. Not only had they forfeited the chance of some attractive cup ties but, more importantly, they were in danger of losing some of their best players who were being offered inducements by other clubs to join them.

A number of crisis meetings were held at St Jude's Institute to try and find a way out of the situation. Some of the committee members felt that professionalism was the solution, arguing that if the players were paid, they would stay. But others were strongly opposed to this, firmly believing that football should be played for fun not for profit. Payment of players, they felt, would alter the entire character and ethos of the game. Inevitably there was much heated discussion but eventually, on 18 December 1898, the supporters of professionalism had their way. The momentous decision was taken not only to turn professional but also to become a limited company with a board of directors. Ten days later, on 28 December, The Queen's Park Rangers

Football and Athletic Club, Limited was formally registered. It was a radical decision and caused great dissension. Some of the players left in protest, not at all impressed by the lure of money. But professionalism had arrived and it was at the club to stay. For all the arguments against it, it was to prove the springboard that was to launch the club to great heights. Queen's Park Rangers Football Club would one day join the élite of English football.

Of course, the change of status to a limited company meant that the club could no longer use St Jude's Institute as its headquarters. Sidney Bott had made this facility available to Rangers for 13 years but it was not possible for the arrangement to continue. The club would have to find another administrative base to register as its official headquarters. It was George Mousell, the new secretary, who came up with a location for the club's office – his home at 89 Lancefield Street close to St Jude's Church.

The continuing link with the founder members

The member of the original St Jude's team who seems to have played the longest for Rangers was Tom Handford who was still scoring goals in the 1895–96 season. However, when their playing days were over, many of the founder members maintained a close relationship with the club. George Wodehouse never lost touch with it and, in fact, he became a director in 1924 when he was 56. Even after he had left the Queen's Park Estate and moved to Harrow, he remained very closely involved with Rangers until his death in 1947 at the age of 79. But the Wodehouse link with the club remained a very long one as George's son, also called George, followed in his father's footsteps by playing for Rangers and then becoming a director. Albert Pearsall, too, became a director and was in fact vice-chairman for 16 years until his death in 1946 at the age of 72.

But what of the two founders of St Jude's Institute FC, Jack McDonald and Fred Weller? After they had finished playing, they followed the fortunes of Rangers very closely but, sadly, Jack McDonald did not witness the club's great Southern League championship successes of 1908 and 1912 because of his tragically early death in his thirties. Fred Weller, on the other hand, enjoyed a very long life. He never left the Queen's Park Estate, living with his wife, Mary, and their four children (two daughters and two sons) first at 34 Farrant

Street then at 29 Huxley Street. Weller died at Paddington Hospital on 29 November 1955 at the ripe old age of 88. He had worked as a carpenter for the whole of his life, eventually attaining the position of foreman carpenter with the Great Western Railway.

Of course, there would probably be no Queen's Park Rangers Football Club at all had the Revd Sidney Bott not had the vision to erect St Jude's Institute in the heart of the Queen's Park Estate. Although St Jude's itself was demolished in 1961, the Institute building – now called St Jude's Hall – still proudly stands at the corner of Ilbert Street and Fourth Avenue. Its external appearance has hardly changed since it opened its doors in 1884. Supporters of Queen's Park Rangers could pause here and spare a moment's thought for people like Jack McDonald, Fred Weller and the Revd Charles Young who have given them so much.

9

Southampton

———•◆•———

On Saturday 19 May 2001 Southampton Football Club played Arsenal in the last match of the season. It was also the last match at The Dell, home of the club since 1898. Fittingly, the occasion was marked by a 3–2 victory for Southampton, Matt Le Tissier scoring the winner in the 89th minute. Three months later, on Saturday 18 August 2001, Southampton played Spanish club Espanyol in a friendly to mark the opening of their new stadium called The Friends Provident St Mary's Stadium. 'What's in a name?' asked Juliet in one of Shakespeare's most famous plays. In the case of Southampton's new home, a great deal. Southampton Football Club was founded at St Mary's Church, Southampton, and the name of the new stadium reflects this fact. Indeed, the club was once called Southampton St Mary's after the church, and from the 'St' in 'St Mary's' came the nickname 'The Saints'. Appropriately, then, the clergyman who led the service of blessing that preceded the match with Espanyol was the rector of St Mary's Church.

The parish of St Mary's

Southampton Football Club came into being as a result of the response made by St Mary's to the needs of the parish in the 1880s. And those needs were many and great. Until the early 1840s the Southampton area had been largely agricultural, but with the coming of the London & South Western Railway in 1840 and the opening of the docks in 1842 all that changed. The farming population was slowly replaced by dock labourers and seamen, and agricultural land made way for vast tracts of terraced housing. Where there had once been wide-open spaces, by the 1880s there was overcrowding and squalor. There was also considerable poverty. Wages were low and work was not always guaranteed, and inevitably other social problems such as drink, crime and prostitution arose. And the man destined to become the club's first president, the rector of St Mary's, Canon Basil Wilberforce, knew these conditions only too well – in the vast slum districts of his parish between the church and the River Itchen lived Southampton's most socially deprived inhabitants.

Canon Basil Wilberforce, the club's first president

Albert Basil Orme Wilberforce – he was always known simply as Basil Wilberforce – was born in Winchester in 1841 into an illustrious family. He was the grandson of the renowned politician and philanthropist William Wilberforce who led the movement that brought about the abolition of the slave trade in the British Empire, and the son of Samuel Wilberforce, the Bishop of Oxford who helped keep the Church of England intact after a number of its leading members had joined the Roman Catholic Church. He was also the godson of Queen Victoria. He was educated at Eton College, the country's top school, and at Exeter College in the University of Oxford. With such a pedigree, the contrast with his present environment could not have been more marked.

Although there were some fairly affluent shopkeepers living in the St Mary's parish, the vast majority of Wilberforce's parishioners were severely impoverished. In Victorian times, however, it was not unusual for people of a privileged background to worship at, and serve in, a church in a deprived area. The sense of mission among highly respectable and wealthy Christians to the poor was strong, and many members of the congregation of St Mary's who did not live in the locality were pleased to devote time, money and energy to serving those less privileged than themselves. Of course, it would be wrong to claim that all those attending the church were motivated by lofty ideals. As the mother church of Southampton, St Mary's enjoyed considerable prestige as the venue for important municipal functions, such as the induction of the mayor. No doubt some members of the congregation were attracted there simply because it was the place to be seen.

Wilberforce, however, would have found this repugnant. He clearly stated that he did not consider churchgoing as such to be the defining characteristic of a Christian. In his writings he was constantly at pains to stress that a Christian was a person who enjoyed a personal relationship with Christ. He emphasized this in the parish magazine of January 1888: 'Personal fellowship with Christ is then the secret of quietness and peace amongst brethren. In like manner it is the source of heart rest in the difficulties of life. To be a Christian is not to profess a faith, or to conform to a creed, it is the acknowledgement of a close connection between Christ and the soul; it is not the imitation of a perfect model, but the indwelling of a spiritual power.'

And Wilberforce himself certainly needed 'the indwelling of a spiritual power' to help him in his struggle against the enormous social problems that confronted him within his 'difficult needy Parish', as he called it in the July 1894 parish magazine. As a forceful advocate of total abstinence from alcohol, for instance, he had to endure what he described in the parish magazine of October 1887 as 'the torrent of abuse poured upon me by angry liqueur dealers and their clients' who were not sympathetic to his view that alcohol was a cause of much social misery.

Others attacked him for not doing enough. One incensed correspondent to a local newspaper trumpeted that Wilberforce ought to realize 'that the immediate neighbourhood of his church and residence are groaning under the curse of drunkenness and immorality; THAT A STREET IMMEDIATELY OPPOSITE HIS CHURCH TEEMS WITH BROTHELS; THAT THE PUBLIC FOOTPATH THROUGH HIS CHURCHYARD IS THE NIGHTLY RESORT OF PROSTITUTES who solicit, aye, and ply their vile calling there'. Instead of taking offence at these words, Wilberforce quoted them in the October 1887 issue of the parish magazine in support of his call for immediate action: 'Let me commend the words printed in small capitals to the attention of the Magistrates and Watch Committee of this town. Strip them of their obvious exaggeration, and there is enough truth in them to make every professed Christian in S. Mary's throw aside indifference and guilty acquiescence and plunge into God's battle.'

In fact, St Mary's had already plunged into God's battle. Under Wilberforce's leadership the church responded to the social problems that were rife in the parish by forming numerous organizations targeting specific needs. The parish magazines show that these included temperance clubs encouraging abstinence from alcohol; a working men's club that provided wholesome recreational activities, including cricket and rowing, as an alternative to the public house; a night school 'for a rough and neglected class of lads'; a club 'for working lads'; and a mothers' group. For the poor and hungry of the parish St Mary's ran three soup kitchens and organized a special treat at Christmas. There were also Sunday Schools for the teaching of Scripture and basic literacy skills. But the organization that is of most interest to supporters of Southampton FC is the St Mary's Young Men's Association. It was the cradle of their club.

The Young Men's Association

The Young Men's Association (YMA) was formed at St Mary's in or around 1881 for young men aged between 15 and 22. (It is not to be confused with the Young Men's Christian Association (YMCA) which is an entirely separate organization.) The primary purpose of the YMA was 'aiding the spiritual life, not omitting with this the manly exercises of the physical life'. An article in the March 1886 issue of the parish magazine pointed out that 'All connected with the club are believers in muscular Christianity, and think that the advantage of strong developed limbs, a supple frame, and a quick eye, cannot be overestimated.' YMA members were expected to attend Bible classes and to engage in parish duties. These could be teaching in the Sunday Schools, involvement in some kind of mission activity (perhaps with the 'rough and neglected' lads) or singing in the choir.

The YMA was a vibrant organization offering a variety of activities to which the parish magazine gave regular coverage. Activities ranged from athletics, cricket and gymnastics to membership of a choral society. There were lectures on subjects of topical interest and there was a reading room for those who wished to do some quiet reading. The membership was drawn principally, if not wholly, from the middle class and was not, therefore, representative of the inhabitants of the parish.

The birth of the football club

In November 1885 an important step was taken by members of the YMA cricket club: they met together at the Grove Street Schoolrooms to discuss the formation of a football club. The meeting was chaired by the curate of St Mary's and leader of the YMA, the Reverend Arthur Baron Sole. The outcome was to prove historic. According to

Francis Montgomery, who was present, it was decided 'to form a club known as the St Mary's Association Football Club. This being carried, my old college colours, red and white, were chosen.' In fact, Montgomery didn't get it quite right. The club was actually named The St Mary's Young Men's Association Football Club. In time, Montgomery would serve as its secretary and become a vice-president. And Southampton FC, who emerged from this club, still play in the colours of Montgomery's old college, St John's in London.

Arthur Sole, who chaired that historic meeting, joined the clergy of St Mary's as a curate in 1878 at the age of 22. A keen sportsman himself with a particular talent for swimming and yachting, it is not surprising that he was happy to be involved in a meeting that launched a new sports club. However, he did not remain long enough to watch the football club grow, leaving St Mary's for St Thomas's, Winchester, only a few months after chairing the meeting that had launched the club. As rector of St Thomas's he continued to promote the value of physical recreation by setting up a gymnasium and running an annual camp with a sports emphasis. After his move to Winchester, Sole did not completely lose touch with the St Mary's football club. When St Mary's beat Christchurch in the final of the Hampshire Junior Cup at Winchester in April 1889, he welcomed some 50 of their players and supporters for tea at St Thomas's rectory after the match.

Although it was Arthur Sole who chaired the meeting that gave birth to the St Mary's YMA Football Club, it was the rector, Basil Wilberforce, who was invited to become the club's first president. He was to hold this position for the next nine years. Wilberforce was not involved in the day-to-day running of the club but he did show his support for it by presenting annual awards to the YMA footballers (and cricketers). Wilberforce was not known to have had any particular sporting interests but he enthusiastically embraced the 'muscular Christian' movement that was responsible for the widespread growth of football clubs in churches throughout the country. He was a great admirer of the writings of Charles Kingsley, the Hampshire clergyman who was the driving force behind the movement, and Wilberforce was responsible for the appearance of many of Kingsley's sermons in the parish magazine. The muscular Christian movement was in full swing by the 1880s, and it was in this climate that the YMA Football Club was born at St Mary's.

The first matches

The fledgling club played its first game on Saturday 21 November 1885 at the County Cricket Ground. Their opponents were Freemantle FC, a club associated with nearby Christ Church, whose curate, the Reverend George D'Arcy, was a prominent Freemantle player. The honours that day went to St Mary's YMA, who ran out easy 5–1 winners, Charles Bromley scoring a hat-trick and Arthur Fry, the captain, scoring twice. It is not absolutely certain who the St Mary's players were in that historic first match, but the probable line-up, based on recollections of members of the side, was: Ralph Ruffell, George Muir, R. McDonnell, A. G. Fry, Charles Deacon, A. Gandy, Arthur A. Fry, George Gandy, Charles Bromley, George McIvor, and A. Varley. They were predominantly, if not wholly, educated men and in terms of social background would have had little in common with the vast majority of the residents of the St Mary's parish.

During that first season, 1885–86, the club is known from press reports to have played at least eight matches, winning five, drawing one, and losing two. Results in the second season were also encouraging, with only two defeats in 13 games. But the successes of the first two seasons could hardly be attributed to a settled side – 37 players were used in the 15 matches for which team lists have been located. One of the players who turned out for the club in its second season was the Reverend Charles Edwyn Jackson, who was a curate at St Mary's from 1884 until 1888. He was also the sub-warden of the YMA.

The first trophy

All matches played in the club's first two seasons were friendlies, but in 1887–88 a cup competition was entered for the first time. It was the newly constituted Hampshire FA Junior Cup and St Mary's YMA were one of 18 clubs participating. YMA got off to a promising start, beating Totton away 1–0. A massive 10–0 win against Petersfield in the second round at the Antelope Cricket Ground (which was to become the club's regular home) sent aspirations soaring, and buoyed by their success against Petersfield, YMA sent Lymington crashing out 4–0 in the third round at Redbridge. It was back to Southampton for the semi-final at the County Cricket Ground, where Bournemouth Arabs provided the opposition. In a closely contested match, YMA squeezed through to the final, narrowly winning 2–1. And so, the stage was set for the final against Southampton Harriers at the County Cricket Ground on 10 March 1888.

Exactly one week before this historic encounter, St Mary's YMA had beaten Cowes 1–0 in a friendly. There is nothing remarkable about the opposition or the result, but the game is memorable because of the match report that appeared in *The Southampton Times & Hampshire Express*. It was the first time that the local press referred to St Mary's YMA as 'The Saints', and in doing so, it gave birth to a nickname that has been attached to its offspring, Southampton Football Club, ever since.

The Saints took the field against Southampton Harriers on 10 March hoping to go home with their first ever trophy, but a 2–2 draw meant that the sides would have to meet again. The replay took place a fortnight later on 24 March at the County Ground in front of an estimated crowd of 600. And it was to be a red-letter day for the team from St Mary's. Their 2–1 victory against the Harriers was to be the club's first taste of glory. It would not be their last.

The church and the spirit of the club

A celebration dinner was held a week later at Gidden's Restaurant, a hostelry popular among the sporting fraternity. A glowing tribute appeared in the pages of the April issue of the St Mary's parish magazine: 's. MARY'S FOOTBALL CLUB. – We are glad to record a great triumph for the above Club, which has now, by following up its many victories won the much coveted "Cup" for the year. We cordially congratulate them on their success.' The church was certainly pleased with the success of its football team, but a closer look at this brief report will reveal that there is more to it than meets the eye.

From the very beginning, the club had enjoyed the full backing of the church. A curate of the church had presided at its launch, another had played for it, the rector was its president, the parish magazine reported on its progress. But the above report of the Hampshire Junior Cup success was unusual. For the first time, the club's full title was not used – the 'YMA' had been dropped. Significantly, these letters also disappeared in newspaper reports at about the same time. But why?

The reason for this sudden change of name remains a mystery. One guess might be that the club was recruiting players from across the church as a whole, not just from the YMA, hence the more general title 'St Mary's Football Club'. Perhaps this is why Canon Wilberforce was happy to continue as its president? Another possible explanation can be inferred from an item that appeared in the October 1887 issue of the parish magazine indicating that all was not well at the Young Men's Association, of which the football club was a part. The committee was concerned that many YMA members were not taking the conditions of membership seriously enough, and felt that the time had come to take a hard line. The following statement in the parish magazine was unequivocal:

> It has been decided by the committee that members absenting them-selves from every Bible class for a fortnight, without written excuse, shall receive a communication from the secretary, and upon further silence of another week, shall be understood to have withdrawn from the Association.
>
> It has also been decided that 'The Association' shall in future con-sist only of those engaged in Parochial Church Work (viz., Choir or Sunday School teaching).

Could it be that the deletion of the 'YMA' from the football club's title was the result of many of its members ignoring the above warning?

There is another clue to suggest this might be the case. On 23 January 1888, some three months after the warning had appeared in the parish magazine, Canon Wilberforce took the chair at an impor-tant meeting of YMA members. The meeting began on a relaxed enough note with presentations by Wilberforce to two players in the YMA football club, George Gandy and Ralph Ruffell, and one in the cricket club, Walter Farenden. Once the presentations were over, the serious business began. It was a debate on getting the YMA back to basics as it was clearly no longer fulfilling its proper function. The question those present were asked to consider was: 'How to restore the Association to its proper position and primary purpose of aiding the spiritual life, not omitting with this the manly exercises of the physical life.'

The outcome was a decision very similar to the statement put out by the committee of the YMA three months earlier. The meeting unanimously decided 'That the S. Mary's Church of England Young

Men's Association should, in future, consist only of members who are either active workers in some branch of the parochial organization, or regular attendants at one of the Bible classes.' And to make a clean sweep of things, it was further decided that only members of the association who agreed to enrol anew on this understanding would be allowed to continue in membership. Did too few of the football players satisfy the association's membership conditions for the letters 'YMA' to continue to be valid in its title?

Progress on the pitch

Whatever distractions there may have been off the pitch, performances on it were clearly unaffected. Having won the Hampshire Junior Cup in 1887–88, Saints did so again the following two seasons, and, in recognition of their three successive triumphs in the competition, they were allowed to keep the trophy permanently. Such was the growing strength of the club that in 1889–90 it not only won the Junior Cup for the third time, but also went through the whole season unbeaten.

Not surprisingly, the Saints decided to step up a level the following season, 1890–91, and they duly entered the Hampshire Senior Cup. It proved to be a good decision. They easily made their way through to the final at the County Cricket Ground where their opponents were to be the Aldershot-based Royal Engineers, winners of the trophy the previous two seasons. Between three and four thousand spectators were drawn to the County Ground in anticipation of a stirring encounter between these two giants of Hampshire football and the occasion was marked by the publication for the first time of a match programme. (In those days it was in the form of a card.) To the delight of the Saints' supporters, their team overcame the mighty Engineers by three goals to one to take the trophy from them.

Inspired by this success, the club set its sights even higher and in the 1891–92 season entered the prestigious FA Cup competition. In the first qualifying round an impressive 4–1 away win against Bristol club Warmley set the stage for the first ever FA Cup tie to take place in the city of Southampton: Saints had been drawn at home against Reading. It was an unforgettable occasion. To the delight of the St Mary's supporters, their team was in scintillating form that day, thrashing Reading 7–0. But their joy was short-lived as Saints were not permitted to progress to the next round. It had emerged that two of their players, both recruited only a fortnight previously, were ineligible to play. St Mary's were disqualified from the competition. It was a massive disappointment but there was still something left to cheer about at the end of the season. On 12 March, Saints met the Army Medical Staff in the final of the Hampshire Senior Cup and won convincingly 5–0. This victory ensured a fifth successive season with a trophy.

The move to professionalism

Confidence was riding high. Consistent success on the field was accompanied by a rapid growth in membership, which by the 1892–93 season had reached a record high of 600. And success on the field fuelled even greater ambition. The club was now eager to compete with the best, although it was fairly obvious that it could only do so by improving the quality of its playing staff. It was time, therefore, to change the recruiting policy. And so, in the summer of 1892, Jack Dollin of Freemantle AFC became the first player to sign for St Mary's on professional terms – albeit secretly! His services were secured for a wage of £1 per week and a job thrown in. Until now, as F. G. Ryder, a former Freemantle player, recalled many years later, 'The players who became St Mary's were a "close-styled" little body; all connected with the mother parish in some way.' In the seven years of the club's existence there had been only a gradual turnover of players, but, after the signing of Dollin, the turnover was rapid.

In 1892–93, Saints again reached the final of the Hampshire Senior Cup but this time there was to be no trophy. In front of an enthusiastic crowd of more than 6,000 packed into the County Ground, they succumbed 2–1 to Freemantle. A few weeks later, on 26 April, they had the chance to redeem the season and make a real name for themselves. A prestigious friendly match had been arranged at the County Ground against Stoke, a team playing in the First Division of the Football League (then the highest level of English football). Saints could now measure themselves against the best. And they fell short. An 8–0 thrashing shattered any illusions they may have had about being ready to join the élite. They were not yet good enough.

New blood was needed in the team. Advertising in the athletic press had already been tried, but had only produced one player of note, Jack Dorkin. The recruitment drive was intensified in 1893–94 and three more professionals were added to the ranks. Despite injuries to key players, the season was reasonably successful with appearances in three local cup finals.

Wilberforce succeeded by Bencraft as president

The next season was a watershed in the history of the club. There were two major changes, one off and one on the field. First, there was a change in the presidency. Canon Basil Wilberforce, who had been rector of St Mary's since 1871, left Southampton in June 1894 for London to take up an appointment as Canon Residentiary of Westminster Abbey. (Two years later, in 1896, he was to become Chaplain of the House of Commons.) His contribution to the development of the club should not be underestimated. There can be little doubt that, as an adherent of the muscular Christian movement, he had created the climate and conditions at St Mary's that made it possible for a football club to be formed and to flourish there. Furthermore, he had identified with the club in a very real way by allowing his name to be associated with it as president, and he had given it another very obvious seal of approval by allowing it to play with the name of the church in its title.

Wilberforce's successor as president was Dr Russell Bencraft. Bencraft had very close associations with St Mary's Church throughout his life. As a boy he had spent many happy hours on the Deanery sports field close to the rectory, and as a young man he had taught in the Sunday School. He was later a sidesman of the church and a regular reader of the lessons at services. He had been a stalwart of the Young Men's Association from its earliest days and a prominent figure in its football club from the start. Although he had only turned out as a player on one occasion in a friendly, he played a key role on the committee and fronted social occasions. Such was his stature and influence in the club that *The Southampton Times* mistakenly referred to him as 'the president' in its report of the annual dinner in May 1891.

Bencraft was a good all-round sportsman. He played cricket for Hampshire and became a member of the MCC committee. He won prizes as an amateur oarsman and on the running track, he was a good horseman and cyclist, he was a fine rugby player and he was even handy with a billiard cue. He became president of the Hampshire Football Association, the Southern Football League, the Hampshire Rugby Union and the Stoneham Golf Club.

He was to become one of the most prominent citizens of Southampton, achieving distinction in both his medical career and in business. He was also a benefactor of numerous charities. In 1924 he was awarded a knighthood. Wilberforce would have been well aware of the calibre of this man and it no doubt greatly reassured him to know that the presidency of the football club would be in such safe hands after his departure for Westminster.

Membership of the Southern League

The second major development was on the playing side. The club had come a long way since the early days of casual friendlies. After repeated cup successes, the time had come to join a league. St Mary's duly applied for membership of the newly formed Southern League for the start of the 1894–95 season, but their application was initially rejected. However, the decision was reversed when the 2nd Scots Guards withdrew. This was truly the end of one era and the start of another, symbolically marked by the retirement of goalkeeper Ralph Ruffell – the last remaining member of the YMA team – and another change of name, St Mary's Football Club becoming Southampton St Mary's Football Club.

Southampton St Mary's first match in the Southern League took place at home at the Antelope Cricket Ground on 6 October 1894 against Chatham. A crowd of between 4,000 and 5,000 turned up to sample league football there for the first time. And they were not disappointed. Saints, with eight professionals in their side, proved too strong for the wholly amateur Chatham club, winning the match 3–1. It was a good start to what proved to be a successful season. St Mary's finished in third place in the league, won the Hampshire Senior Cup for the third time, and battled through four qualifying rounds of the FA Cup to reach the first round proper for the first time.

The club was enjoying its success and was hungry for more. Its early days as a church team playing purely for fun were rapidly becoming a distant memory. More and more professionals were being signed and by 1895–96 the playing strength was such that the reserve team was considered good enough to be entered in the Hampshire Senior Cup. It duly reached the final.

At the end of the 1895–96 season, Saints found themselves without a ground. For many years they had played their home matches at the Antelope Cricket Ground, which was on land owned by St Mary's Church. But in the summer of 1896 the church needed funds to provide an income for Canon Wilberforce's successor, who, unlike Wilberforce, was not a man of private means. The church decided that the best way to raise the necessary funds was to sell the cricket ground. It was duly sold to builders for development and the Saints had to look elsewhere for a home. They managed to find a temporary base for the start of the 1896–97 season at the Hampshire County Cricket Ground and quite clearly enjoyed playing there: they won the Southern League championship without losing a single match. Appropriately, perhaps, the championship shield was presented to the club by Dr Bencraft, president of both the club and the league.

Change of name to Southampton Football Club

That was to be the last season in which the club played with the name of St Mary's Church in its title. There were many who felt that the present name was too parochial for a club that had clearly outgrown its roots and they argued that it was time to move forward as a limited company under a new name – Southampton Football Club. There were murmurs in the press that the deletion of 'St Mary's' from the title would result in the loss of the nickname 'The Saints' but other than this there were no voices raised in opposition. At the annual general meeting on 11 June 1897 the momentous decision was taken to form a limited liability company called The Southampton Football and Athletic Company Limited.

After playing under the name St Mary's for 12 years, the link with the church was now formally broken. With Dr Bencraft's resignation as president, the symbolic link between the church and the presidency also ceased. Bencraft continued, however, to take a close interest in the club and he attended as many matches as he could. Although there was also to be some continuity in personnel between the St Mary's club and its successor – George Muir, for instance, played in the original team of 1885 and was a director of Southampton FC from 1915 until 1936 – the club/church link was now officially over. It is ironic, therefore, that the nickname 'The Saints' lived on.

The next important step for the members of the newly re-constituted club was to find a permanent home. They did not have too long to wait. Just twelve months later, George Thomas, one of the club's directors, found what he thought would be the ideal site. It was a former wooded hollow with a stream at its bottom – a dell – that had been excavated by the Didcot, Newbury & Southampton Railway for use as a goods siding. It was less than 200 yards from the County Ground. The land was duly acquired and converted into a football ground, appropriately nicknamed 'The Dell'. This name would be synonymous with the club for the next 103 years until it moved again in 2001. Which, of course, is where we came in . . .

10

Swindon Town

————•◆•————

'Town have made another signing in their bid to climb up the division one table. The Rev. Simon Stevenette joined the club at the tail-end of last week as their new chaplain.' Those words in *The Swindon Advertiser* in November 1998 signified that Swindon Town Football Club, in a very real sense, had returned home. Their new club chaplain had been installed only the previous month as vicar of Christ Church, and it was a former Christ Church clergyman, the Reverend William Baker Pitt, who in 1879 founded Swindon Town Football Club. On Pitt's departure from Swindon in 1882, the formal link between church and club was broken but almost 120 years later, with the appointment of the new vicar of Christ Church as club chaplain, it was restored. Significantly, the club was represented by vice-chairman Cliff Puffett at the service in which the Revd Stevenette was officially installed as vicar of Christ Church. Puffett explained to the press: 'We need all of the help we can get, not only financially and practically, but also spiritually.'

Christ Church, known affectionately as 'The Old Lady on the Hill', is a magnificent structure with a soaring spire situated in Swindon's Old Town. It was designed by the eminent Victorian architect George Gilbert Scott, the man responsible for the design of the Albert Memorial in London. The foundation stone of Christ Church was laid in 1850 and the building opened for worship the following year. From the churchyard behind the east end there is a clear view of the County Ground, the home of Swindon Town Football Club. Conversely, the church is also in clear view of Swindon Town supporters as they exit the stadium after a match. The visual link between the church and the club is probably taken for granted but thanks to Pitt there is a much closer and more meaningful connection between these two prominent Swindon landmarks. It is one worth exploring.

The founder of the club

The story begins on 18 January 1856 when William Baker Pitt was born in Exeter. His father, Thomas, had a profitable grocery business there. By 1861 the family was sufficiently well off to be able to employ a cook and a male servant and to engage a governess for five-year-old William. Pitt did not want to follow in his father's footsteps but chose instead to become an Anglican clergyman. After attending the London College of Divinity he was ordained a deacon of the Church of England in 1879 and that same year he took up an appointment as curate of Christ Church in Swindon. Lodgings were arranged for him in the town at the home of a local grocer, Frederick Osman, who lived with his wife, Mary, at 38 Belle Vue Road. They were probably business acquaintants of Pitt's father.

It was a brave decision on the part of 23-year-old Pitt to accept the position of curate at Christ Church. He was probably fully aware that he was coming into a parish that had gained the reputation of being a very turbulent one. It may have alarmed him to read in an article in *The Swindon Advertiser* of 29 March 1879 that 'The circumstances attending the leaving of curate after curate are too vividly remembered in the town to need recapitulation.' He may also have noticed in the same article that the Bishop of Gloucester and Bristol, Dr Charles Ellicott, regarded Christ Church as 'the one black spot' in his diocese. It seems that the reason for the unsettled state of affairs was the controversial vicar of Christ Church, Henry Baily, an outspoken man who frequently crossed swords with powerful figures in the community. Among his enemies were the local MP and Lord of the Manor, Ambrose Goddard, and the owner of *The Swindon Advertiser*, William Morris. However, it is fair to say that Baily was not one to take up cudgels lightly: he did so only if he felt that the best interests of his parishioners were threatened. But once provoked to act, he was not afraid to say exactly what he thought.

The club is born

Around the time Pitt arrived at Christ Church, there was a heavily charged atmosphere as Baily and the Bishop, Dr Ellicott, had been involved in an exchange of correspondence in the local press disagreeing on an important matter of principle. But despite the seeming cauldron that Pitt had entered, he quickly settled in and established a good working relationship with Baily. He became a very popular figure in the parish, especially among young people, who looked upon him with great affection and respect. One of the organizations with which he became actively involved was the Young Men's Christian Association (YMCA) and he did much good work on its behalf. Pitt related easily to others and one of his great gifts was the ability to bridge the divide between people who were not well disposed towards each other. In the Swindon of the time there was plenty of opportunity to exercise this gift.

Division between different parts of Swindon had developed after the arrival of the Great Western Railway (GWR) in the 1830s. In 1801 the little market town had a population of just under 1,200 but when the renowned Victorian engineer, Isambard Kingdom Brunel, established the GWR engineering works, there was such an influx of workers that by the 1850s the housing and other amenities that had been built to accommodate them had grown into a town bigger than the original Old Town on the hill. By 1864 the total population of Swindon had grown to over 7,000 and separate councils were set up for the old and new parts. By the time Pitt arrived in 1879 the total population of Swindon had soared to about 19,000 with a clear physical division between Old and New Town. And the division was more than just physical: it was also mirrored by a mutual suspicion between the residents of the separate communities. But just as Pitt was able to rise above the difficulties at a church that was 'the one black spot' in the diocese, so, too, was he able to form a bridge between Old and New Swindon. He achieved this through football, a game that he loved.

In the autumn of 1879 Pitt met with some youthful employees of the GWR works who lived in New Town to discuss the formation of a football club. The meeting took place at the King William Street School in Old Town only a few minutes' walk from Christ Church. Significantly, Pitt, a leading figure in Old Town, had succeeded in getting the young men from New Town to cross the divide. A lively and purposeful discussion took place in the school building (which still stands) and the outcome was an enthusiastic response to Pitt's proposal to form a club. It was agreed by all present to call it Swindon Town Football Club and to play according to Association rules. As only the second club in the region to choose to play this version of the game – the other was Marlborough – it would not be easy at first to find opponents but as Association football was rapidly beginning to spread through England, this situation would soon change.

The first match

The first recorded match played by Pitt and his youthful enthusiasts took place on Saturday 29 November 1879 against Rover FC at the latter's ground. Pitt's club was so new that the match report in the local press two weeks later did not get its title quite right, referring to it as 'Swindon Association F.C.' This historic first match ended in a disappointing 4–0 defeat but it did not help that Swindon fielded only ten players against Rover FC's 11. Despite the size of the defeat three members of the Swindon team, including Pitt, played well and were singled out for special mention: 'For the visitors Messrs. Pitt, Cockbill, and Watson rendered good service'. Playing in a 1-2-6 formation that day, the team line-up was: R. H. Barnett, captain (goal); W. Woolford (full-back); A. Watson, G. Rawlings (half-backs); while the six forwards were Revd W. B. Pitt and C. Humphreys, (right); T. Hancock and W. Cockbill (centre); and Davies and J. Cook (left).

A change of name and early homes

After this match against Rover FC, there are no reports in the press of any further games until about a year later. In the meantime, the club had changed its name. In a memorable speech celebrating the club's Southern League championship success and reported in *The Swindon Advertiser* of 22 September 1911, Pitt explained why: 'we decided to call our club the Swindon Town Football Club. But we found that that was rather a large mouthful to shout out, and we afterwards changed the name to the Spartan Club.' The first match played under the new name was on 18 December 1880 against Mr Price's XI, the result being a 1–0 win for the Spartans. W. Keylock was the scorer of the goal and he can, therefore, rightly claim to be the first known goalscorer in Swindon Town FC's history. It was probably also Pitt's first match as captain, as R. H. Barnett seems to have left the club after the Rover game.

Spartans are known to have played two more matches in the 1880–81 season, a 0–0 draw against St Mark's Young Men's Friendly

Society on 12 February 1881 and a 2–1 win in the return match with Mr Price's XI on 12 March, although for some unknown reason, Pitt did not feature in either. In his 1911 speech Pitt recalled that the games were played on 'a field opposite the Wharf, and kindly lent to us by Mr Hooper Deacon, who is always a friend of sport'. The field in question was very near to the County Ground where the club plays today.

The following season was to be Pitt's last as he was to leave Christ Church in 1882 to take up an appointment as rector of All Saints, Liddington, about six miles away. Of the seven recorded matches played by Spartans in 1881–82, Pitt featured in three of them, including the 2–2 draw against St Mark's Young Men's Friendly Society on 12 November 1881. This match has assumed great significance in the club's history because of the long-held belief that the Spartans and St Mark's merged immediately afterwards to form Swindon Town Football Club. As a result, 1881 became accepted as the club's official foundation date and the centenary was duly celebrated in 1981. However, in the light of the discovery of the match report against Rover FC and Pitt's own recollections in his 1911 speech, there can be no doubt that 1879 was the actual foundation year. Furthermore, the Spartans never merged with St Mark's YMFS. Match reports in *The Swindon Advertiser* reveal that Spartans played St Mark's once again that season (28 January) and twice more the following season. And St Mark's YMFS were still playing as an independent club until at least the 1891–92 season, by which time they were fielding 'A' and 'B' teams.

The club continued to play as the Spartan Club for one more season, 1882–83. In the three seasons as the Spartans, the club had various homes. After first playing at Hooper Deacon's field, a switch was made to J. E. G. Bradford's field next to a quarry in Old Town. It was not an inspired choice. Exuberant play – or lack of skill – often resulted in the ball being kicked into the quarry from where it could not easily be retrieved. This must have been extremely frustrating and also quite costly as footballs were not cheap at the time. But the need to move to a safer home became a matter of extreme urgency when a spectator had the great misfortune to disappear into the quarry, probably while attempting to stop the ball. The club then relocated to the Globe Field off what is now Lansdown Road, not far from the King William Street School where Pitt had founded the club. The

Globe Field is now covered with housing but Globe Street and the Globe public house serve as reminders of where the club once played.

Return to the original name and early successes

Before the 1883–84 season began, the club reverted to its original name of Swindon Town Football Club but precisely when or why is not known. Perhaps it was beginning to grow more ambitious and wanted to be representative of the whole town. The first match under the restored name was against Culham College on 20 October 1883 but it was not a very promising start to the season as Swindon went down 2–1. Alfred Cockbill scored the goal. However, after two defeats in the opening three games the team's performances rapidly improved and by the end of the season ten out of the 14 matches had been won. There were some very memorable games including the 6–1 defeat of Wantage, the 7–0 victories against Devizes Depot and old rivals St Mark's YMFS, and the 9–0 battering of VWH Cricklade.

The next season started with another change of ground, the club leaving the Globe Field and playing on a pitch at the Croft. This was to remain their home for the next 11 years. However, as the ground had no changing facilities, a room was made available to the players at the Fountain Inn on nearby Devizes Road from where they had to walk to the ground. There was also little luxury for spectators: to keep their feet dry they had to stand on wooden boards. Nevertheless, the years at the Croft saw the club's first major successes in Wiltshire football. Swindon Town had been doing well in friendly matches, which were the staple diet at the time, but when the Wiltshire Senior Cup was introduced in the 1886–87 season the club virtually made the trophy their own, winning the competition in the first six years of its existence. When they did finally surrender it, the new holders were Swindon Town Reserves!

Major developments

The cup successes showed the growing strength of the club and by 1894 it had progressed sufficiently to employ professionals and to gain admission to the First Division of the newly formed Southern League. However, despite all the progress that had been made, the first season in the Southern League was definitely one to forget.

Swindon finished bottom. Nevertheless, a lot was beginning to happen off the pitch. The following season saw yet another ground move when the Croft was left behind in favour of the County Ground, the team playing on a pitch which is now used for cricket. A year later, in October 1896, Thomas Arkell loaned the club £300 to build a stand on another pitch at the County Ground and this has remained Swindon Town's home until today. Having acquired a permanent ground of its own, the club was in a position to become a limited company and the change of legal status duly occurred in 1897.

Despite the fact that the club was on secure foundations as a limited company with a permanent home, there was very little happening on the pitch to cheer supporters. Performances from 1894–95 until 1907–08 were at best mediocre with the club finishing in the bottom half of the First Division every year but one. However, fortunes began to change in the 1907–08 season when the highest-ever position – fifth – was attained, followed by two successive seasons as runners-up. The breakthrough to national recognition was finally achieved in the brief period from 1910 to 1912 when the club twice reached the semi-finals of the FA Cup and won the First Division championship of the Southern League. These were the club's pre-World War I glory days and they were symbolically marked by the selection of Harold Fleming to play for England, the only man to represent the country while a Swindon Town player.

The legendary Harold Fleming

If there was one man who could be credited with putting the club on the map it was Harold Fleming, known as much for his qualities as a Christian as for his outstanding ability as a footballer. He was a brilliant inside-forward who, in the words of the former Swindon player, Edgar Dawe, 'had the most amazing ball control and body swerve I have ever seen'. According to *The Swindon Advertiser* of 12 February 2004, he was described in his day as 'an artist with the ball, a weaver of patterns with a subtle swerve, and a great goal-getter, always attractive and ever dangerous'. Such was his ability that he was selected to play for England on 11 occasions at a time when international matches were few and far between. Remarkably, only nine of his 11 appearances merited a cap because his two games against Hungary did not count. Continental opposition in those days was not considered good enough to justify the award of a cap. There is no doubt that Fleming would have added to his tally had it not been for the outbreak of World War I.

Fleming was so good that opponents sometimes resorted to violent play in order to try and stop him. In the FA Cup semi-final against Barnsley in 1912 he was so badly injured that he was unable to play for ten months, prompting the *Daily Express* to write: 'Barnsley's treatment of one of the cleanest players who ever donned a football boot was . . . disgraceful. To stop a clever opponent by maiming him is not football.'

Fleming was known throughout the football world for his refusal to play on Good Friday and on Christmas Day – had there been Sunday football he would have refused to play on that day too – but his reputation as a Christian was much more attributable to his gentlemanly conduct on the pitch and to his scrupulous fair play. As one correspondent wrote to *The Swindon Evening Advertiser* following Fleming's death in August 1955, 'his fairness was proverbial.' Another correspondent, writing at the same time, paid the following tribute to Fleming's Christian character: 'It can be said with all truth that he let his light shine before the public. By his life and influence, which radiated over every football ground, he left an indelible impression. Thus he leaves the world a better place for passing through.' It also made a deep impression on Billy Silto, Fleming's room-mate on the England tour of South Africa in 1910, that this great footballer always knelt down humbly to pray before going to bed. Fleming's commitment to young people was another expression of his faith. He would often return to the County Ground when his own training was over to help coach young players and he also devoted many hours working at the youth club at St Mark's Church. Young people loved and respected him and they always referred to him affectionately as 'Our Harold'.

Fleming retired from playing at the age of 37 and eventually opened a sports shop. In his spare time he continued to coach young people, not only at football but also cricket and hockey. More than 50 years after his death at the age of 68 in 1955, his name is still honoured in Swindon. There is a small statue of him at the County Ground with the inscription 'To the inspiring memory of Harold Fleming, the great footballer and gentleman, who played for Swindon Town between 1907–24, and was capped nine times for England.'

His name also lives on in Fleming Way, one of the roads leading from the roundabout at the County Ground.

Pitt, Fleming and the Southern League championship

The Southern League championship success achieved by Fleming and his team-mates gave occasion for a special celebration at the County Ground on Monday 18 September 1911. In front of a crowd of several thousand Swindon supporters, a public presentation of expensive marble clocks was made to each player as a memento of their great achievement. One of the guests of honour was the Revd William Pitt, the club's founder, who was invited to give a speech from the improvised platform on the pitch to the assembled crowd. It was a truly memorable one.

As recorded in *The Swindon Advertiser* of 22 September 1911, Pitt told the audience: 'There is no game I know of which makes such great demands upon judgment, upon courage, and upon endurance, and any game which calls forth and stimulates those qualities I regard as a very good and useful game. I sometimes hear it stated that there is far too much football. I always say there is far too little.' He then referred back to the early days when he founded the club: 'I cannot say that we ever achieved any great results. . . . We always played for the love of the game, and we always played a straight game.' With that statement he clearly alluded to the ethos of the club that prevailed in his day and he drew a significant parallel with the ethos of the club as he saw it now: 'No-one congratulates the team more than I do upon the success which it has achieved. But perhaps there is one thing I congratulate the Club upon more than upon its success, and that is its possession of a personal influence, which I understand makes for sobriety, purity, and the right observance of the Sunday, and I have no hesitation in saying that the success which has attended the team is very largely due to that influence.'

He went on to say that he hoped the club would long retain that influence, stressing that 'a straight life made for a straight kick'. There can be little doubt that the 'influence' to which he was referring was the Christian spirit that was at work in the club. And, equally, there can be little doubt that the member of the side who in his and everyone else's mind exemplified this spirit the most was the great Harold Fleming.

William Pitt's story

Pitt had clearly set a standard at the club when he founded it and it must have given him immense pleasure and satisfaction to see that the tradition of playing 'a straight game' was still alive and well some 30 years later. But what of the story of his own life? How did that unfold?

Having left Christ Church early in 1882, Pitt returned on Wednesday 21 June for his wedding. He was married that day to Alice Mary Kinneir, the daughter of Henry Kinneir, a former church-warden of Christ Church and a respected Swindon solicitor. *The Swindon Advertiser* reports that it was a joyous occasion and one that was warmly celebrated by the parishioners who had not forgotten 'the untiring and Christian spirit in which the bridegroom has carried on his labours in Swindon, particularly amongst the young'. In fact, so popular had Pitt been at Christ Church that the church was packed long before the service was due to begin and the road was crowded by large numbers of people still hoping to get in. The path-way from the church entrance to the road was lined with children from the Sunday School 'all eager in some way or other to show their love for their friends'. It was clear that this man was much loved and would be sorely missed.

When Pitt left Christ Church to take up his appointment as rector of Liddington, he could hardly have guessed that he would remain there for 54 years. His obituary in the local press states that during those years of service he was to earn the reputation as 'a champion of the poor and a practical friend to all in need', working particularly hard to improve the housing conditions of the poor. He also main-tained excellent relationships with young people and was frequently approached by them for advice. The only time he lived away from Liddington in those 54 years was from 1916 to 1917 when he served with the Church Army in France.

He and Alice were to spend a long life together and to know the joys of parenthood, having five children. Alice, their first, was born in 1884, followed by William in 1886, Edith in 1887, Clifford in 1889 and Audrey in 1892. But as well as great joy, they were also to know terrible heartache. The first tragedy they suffered was the death of their youngest son, Clifford, on 1 February 1915 in Baumu, British East Africa. Clifford, an Oxford graduate, had embarked upon a career in colonial administration and seemed destined for great things. But tragically, at the age of 26, he suffered acute sunstroke in Africa and died. His grieving parents placed a memorial window to him in Liddington church in which he is poignantly depicted as a young man in armour sheltering from the sun in the shade of a tree. In 1927 a second memorial window was placed in the church by Pitt and his wife following the death of their only grandson, who was just two years old when he died.

Perhaps the most distressing experience of all was the death of their 45-year-old daughter Alice that occurred in mysterious circumstances on 23 June 1928. Pitt and his wife were away on holiday in Anglesey, North Wales, when the news reached them that Alice's body had been found at the bottom of a well among farm buildings close to the rectory. As Alice had not turned up for lunch, and as there was still no sign of her by mid-afternoon, a search was made for her. When it was discovered that the lid of the well was off, the worst was feared and dragging equipment was fetched. Alice's body was slowly brought to the surface. It was a complete mystery how someone so familiar with the farm and the well could fall into it and die. The coroner's report simply stated 'found drowned in a well, there being no evidence of the state of her mind'. It was a shattering blow for the family and many question marks must long have remained as to the reason for her death.

After 54 years of faithful service in Liddington, Pitt was forced to resign as rector in 1935 because of severe bronchial disorders. He and his wife moved to Bournemouth in the hope that the sea air of the south coast might do him good. But his condition gradually worsened and he suffered long periods of unconsciousness. He finally contracted pneumonia and on 21 November 1936 he died. Four choristers from Liddington church travelled to Bournemouth to bring his body back to Liddington for burial. The funeral took place on 25 November and the Bishop of Malmesbury, who conducted the service, told the congregation that they had lost 'a real kind friend'. Pitt was buried in Liddington churchyard in a grave next to that of his daughter Alice. His wife survived him by seven years but when she died on 17 November 1943 in Braintree, Essex, where she had been living with her daughter, Audrey, her body was brought back to Liddington churchyard for burial with Pitt. They lie facing the west door of the church in a grave marked by a large stone cross.

The club/church link today

Although Pitt left Swindon in 1882 he continued to feel affection long afterwards for the football club he had created there and to be proud of its achievements. But his main concern was that the club should always retain 'that influence' that produced 'a straight life'. He would probably have been delighted, then, to know that the link with Christ Church would one day be restored. He would no doubt also have watched with great pleasure as staff and supporters of Swindon Town – many in club colours – converge on Christ Church for the club's annual Christmas carol service. It is obvious that the 'influence' to which Pitt attached such great importance is alive and well at the club today.

11

Tottenham Hotspur

———•◦•———

Just a short distance from White Hart Lane, the illustrious home of Tottenham Hotspur Football Club, stands All Hallows, the parish church of Tottenham. Its fourteenth-century tower is clearly visible to thousands of Spurs supporters as they make their way in eager anticipation to the stadium on matchdays, but probably no more than a tiny few know of the crucial role the church played in the development of the club they love. Sadly, the historic link between All Hallows and the club has long been forgotten. It is time to tell the fascinating story and to meet some of the remarkable people who were there at the very beginning.

The birth of the club

How did it come about that the parish church of Tottenham was to be instrumental in the formation of one of the most famous football clubs in the world? The story begins one August day in 1882 when a dozen youngsters in their very early teens gathered by a lamp post near the junction of Tottenham High Road and Park Lane to discuss the formation of a football club. One or two attended Tottenham Grammar School, but the rest were pupils at St John's Middle Class School in Tottenham High Road, a school attached to St John's Presbyterian Church. A Scotsman named William Cameron was the headmaster, and such was his devotion to the school that it became known locally simply as 'Mr Cameron's school'. Significantly, most of the schoolboys who met by the lamp post that day were also members of a Bible class run at All Hallows Church by a man who was like a father to them. His name was John Ripsher.

A year or two earlier these boys had formed a cricket club called Hotspur Cricket Club and in their discussion under the lamp post they decided it would be a good idea to form a football club to stay in close touch during the winter months and to keep fit. They gave it the name Hotspur Football Club. Both the cricket and football clubs were called 'Hotspur' because some of the boys had been learning fourteenth-century history at school and had been inspired by the heroic exploits of Sir Henry Percy, who first fought in battle at the age of 14. He was nicknamed 'Harry Hotspur' because he was a reckless fighter (hence 'hot' as in 'hot-headed') and because he usually wore spurs on horseback (hence 'spur'). The choice of name for the two clubs was also quite appropriate for the Tottenham area as the Percy family – the Earls of Northumberland – had once been powerful landowners there, and other names associated with the family such as Percy House, Northumberland Park and the Northumberland Arms were already well established in the locality.

The first four subscriptions to the new Hotspur Football Club were received on 5 September 1882. By the end of September another ten had been added and by the end of the year the total stood at 18. To ensure that as many of the paid-up members as possible could get a game, a line was drawn at this number. Of these 18, 11 were already members of the Hotspur Cricket Club and they have gone down in history as the founder members of the football club. Their names are Robert ('Bobby') Buckle, Hamilton ('Sam') Casey and John ('Jack') Thompson – believed to be the three boys whose idea it was to form a football club – and the brothers John and Tom Anderson, Edward Beaven, Lindsay Casey (brother of Sam), Fred Dexter, Stuart Leaman, Peter Thompson and E(dward?) Wall.

These enterprising boys started out with great enthusiasm. Wanting to become properly organized, they appointed Jack Thompson as secretary and Lindsay Casey as treasurer, while Bobby Buckle and Sam Casey were made captain and vice-captain respectively. However, the club had no premises so the first business meetings took place by candlelight in the shells of houses that were being built in Willoughby Lane or under the light of a gas lamp in Tottenham High Road.

With money from the subscriptions a number of essential items were quickly bought. These included wood from which goal and corner posts could be made, material for corner flags, tape to run from the top of one goalpost to the other (crossbars were not yet in established use), stationery and stamps. They soon found somewhere free to play – the Park Lane end of the Tottenham Marshes – and the father of the Casey brothers saw to it that they had goalposts.

He made them two sets from the wood they had bought and he painted them blue and white. The elder brother of the Caseys (who had suggested the name 'Hotspur' when the cricket club was founded) presented them with their first ball. They could now get started.

During their first season the boys played impromptu friendlies against local teams who fielded players much older than themselves, but the results of only two matches have been traced. One was a 2–0 defeat on 30 September 1882 – the club's first ever match – at the hands of Radicals, the other was an 8–1 thrashing by Latymer.

John Ripsher to the rescue

The enthusiasm that accompanied the birth of the club was soon put to the severest test. Before each home game, the boys took great care in marking out their pitch, but because they were so young they were easy prey for teams of older boys who from time to time would simply push them aside and take over the freshly marked out pitch for themselves. The angry protestations of the Hotspur youngsters were of no avail. They were also frequently subjected to the taunts of bullies who roamed the Marshes on Saturday afternoons looking for trouble. These pressures demoralized them and some of them left the club. After the optimism with which the club had been formed, a spirit of despair now threatened to drive it into extinction. It seemed that it would not survive to play a second season.

In their hour of need the Hotspur boys, in the summer of 1883, turned to someone for help who, they believed, could turn things round. It was John Ripsher, the Bible class teacher at All Hallows Church. Many of the boys attended Ripsher's class at All Hallows, and they had come to love and respect him. In the past he had given them help with their cricket club, so he seemed the obvious person to turn to now.

John Ripsher was born on 3 April 1840 in London at 54 Princes Street, just off Oxford Street and close to Oxford Circus. He was one of five children, four boys and a girl. His father was a linen and woollen draper. However, John did not follow in his father's footsteps, becoming instead a clerk in an iron warehouse. In 1881 he was living with his brother Swann Ripsher and family at Cheriton Villa, Northumberland Park, Tottenham, and he would, therefore, have lived in close proximity to many of the Hotspur boys. Apart from his involvement at All Hallows Church, Ripsher was also a member of the Council of the Tottenham branch of the Young Men's Christian Association (YMCA). This was to play an important part in the club's early history.

The boys had come to the right man. Although the first recorded mention of Ripsher's involvement with the club was a payment of five shillings and threepence (approximately 26p) into its accounts on 30 May 1883, it was the meeting he called in August in a basement kitchen at the YMCA that secured his place in the club's history. Twenty-one boys accepted the invitation to attend, and Ripsher took the chair. The outcome was dramatic. After a lengthy and lively debate, a wholly restructured club with a formally constituted committee was born. Ripsher was elected president and treasurer, Tom Bumberry, Fred Dexter, W. G. Herbert and William ('Billy') Tyrell were elected members of the committee, and Jim Randall and William ('Billy') Harston were appointed captain and vice-captain respectively. The name Hotspur Football Club was retained. It was agreed and entered into the rule book 'that the uniform of the club be navy blue, with scarlet shield on left side of jersey with the letter "H" thereon, and that every member is requested to wear same in matches'.

There is no doubt that this meeting shaped the destiny of the club. Until now its organization had been haphazard and there had been no firm leadership. Youthful enthusiasm alone was not sufficient to ensure its future. With the appearance of Ripsher on the scene, however, everything changed. Under his leadership there was a clear sense of direction and an efficient system of administration. He also secured the YMCA premises as the club's headquarters, providing a base for committee meetings and a place to change on matchdays. It is no wonder, then, that two former players, the writers of the earliest club history in 1908, should state in the book that he was 'the real father and founder of the Tottenham Hotspur Football Club'.

A new spirit at the club

The first match of the 1883–84 season – Saturday 6 October at home against Brownlow Rovers – was a resounding 9–0 victory for Spurs. It was also the first of their matches to receive coverage in the local press. In the return match against Brownlow Rovers later in the season play had to stop ten minutes from time because the ball burst.

The game could not be continued as this was the only ball that Rovers possessed. In those days many clubs could only afford one ball and it had to last the whole season. Hotspur FC, too, had limited funds and sometimes on a Friday there was no match ball for Saturday. When the boys told Ripsher his reply, according to the 1908 history, was always the same: 'Well, never mind, lads, turn up, the Lord will provide.' Sure enough, he himself would turn up the following day with a ball, sometimes two, under his arm – one for practice, one for the match.

It was obvious that a new spirit permeated the club's first season under Ripsher's leadership. This was reflected in the results. Of the 11 known matches played, nine were won and only two lost. Thirty-two goals were scored and only two conceded. But it wasn't just results that were pleasing. The club that had once been losing players because of bullying was now attracting new players from clubs that had been disbanded and was now in the happy position of being able to field a second team. Its results, too, were commendable.

A change of name and headquarters

Although the following season (1884–85) was quite successful on the playing front (18 wins and four draws out of 28 matches) it is remembered for reasons other than football. There were two significant changes. The first was a change of name. It would seem that it was not just the boys of Mr Cameron's school who had been inspired by the exploits of Harry Hotspur. There was another club in London, 'London Hotspur', which also bore the name of this fearless warrior. Not surprisingly, the secretaries of Hotspur FC and London Hotspur frequently received each other's mail. To put an end to this situation, Ripsher's club decided that the most obvious solution was a change of name, and at a meeting of the committee the new name, Tottenham Hotspur Football Club, was adopted.

The second change, unfortunately, was not a welcome one: the club was forced to leave its headquarters at the YMCA with the re-sultant loss of a venue for committee meetings and a changing room for matchdays. This came about as a result of an incident during a practice session one evening in the basement of the YMCA. The boys frequently used the basement for practice, but this particular evening they must have been unusually noisy because they disturbed

a meeting of the YMCA Council on a floor above. One of the coun-
cillors left the meeting and went downstairs to investigate the noise.
But his timing could not have been worse. As he opened the door to
the basement he was hit full in the face by a fierce shot from one
of the players. To make matters worse, the ball had been miskicked into
the fireplace only a few seconds earlier and was covered in soot. To say
that the councillor was displeased to be struck in the face by a soot-
covered ball is an understatement. He returned to the meeting and
angrily reported what had happened. It seems he would be satisfied
with nothing less than the expulsion of the boys from the premises –
permanently! His demand did not fall on deaf ears. The boys had
already blotted their copybook on previous occasions, as club minutes record, by succumbing to the temptation to 'play cards and
sample the mulberries at the end of the garden'. This, it seems, was the
last straw. They had to leave.

For the second time in its short existence the club was in trouble,
and once again it was at All Hallows Church that the Hotspur boys
found friends when they most needed them. It was the vicar, the
Reverend Alexander Wilson, prompted by John Ripsher, who came to
the rescue. Wilson, a Scotsman, became vicar of All Hallows in
September 1870 when he was 56. Prior to his arrival at Tottenham he
had already established a reputation for his concern for the welfare of
young people, having served for some 30 years as secretary of the
lengthily titled Church of England National Society for Promoting
the Education of the Poor in the Principles of the Established
Church. During his term of office, according to his obituary in *The
Weekly Herald* of 4 November 1898, he had achieved great success 'in
covering the country with schools for the poor'. His commitment to
education continued throughout his life. He was active in the development of teacher training establishments to further the quality of
children's education; he was a prolific writer on educational matters;
he was a Diocesan Inspector of Schools; and he was a governor of
Tottenham Grammar School. It is not surprising, in view of his concern for the development of young people, that he should take a keen
interest in Ripsher's work with the boys of the Hotspur Football
Club, especially as many of them were parishioners attending
Ripsher's Bible class at his church. And now Ripsher needed the
vicar's help. The boys had lost their base at the YMCA and urgently
needed new headquarters. Ripsher knew just the place.

A short time before, Wilson, with the help of Ripsher and one of the All Hallows churchwardens, John Thompson, had founded a branch of the Young Men's Church of England Society at 1 Dorset Villas, Northumberland Park. Ripsher saw the premises as the ideal replacement for the YMCA as the club's headquarters. He approached Wilson with the idea. Wilson was no doubt fully aware of the boys' track record at the YMCA and probably had misgivings about the young Hotspur tearaways using the society's premises as their new base. But whatever doubts he may have had, he clearly valued the work Ripsher was doing with the boys and he was quick to give him his support. He was willing to allow the use of 1 Dorset Villas as the club's new headquarters, but on one condition – the boys had to attend All Hallows Church every Wednesday evening. The boys agreed and the move went ahead.

They were very happy there. As one of them wrote in 1908: 'Here we were very comfortable, with library, draughts, chess, cards, dominoes, etc., and we had every encouragement to turn up all week nights, and many a match has been played [tactically planned] over here and plans for future engagements worked out.' It is somewhat surprising that cards were provided for them in view of the fact that card-playing was one of the misdemeanours that had led to their eventual expulsion from the YMCA. It seems that the only facility they lacked at Dorset Villas was a dressing room, but one was made available for them in Somerford Grove a short walk away.

Major developments

Once the important question of new headquarters had been settled, everyone at the club could again concentrate on football. Results went quite well, but it was decided to cancel the last match of the season which had been scheduled for 4 April 1885 in order to watch the FA Cup Final at the Kennington Oval. It was to be contested for the second year running by two of the most famous clubs of the day – Blackburn Rovers and Queen's Park of Glasgow. (Scottish clubs took part in the English FA Cup competition up to the 1886–87 season.) Blackburn won the match 2–0 and the Hotspur boys so admired their stylish play that they decided to abandon their all-blue shirts and adopt the blue and white halved shirts of Blackburn Rovers as the new club colours. The club's symbol, the letter 'H', was sewn on near the left shoulder.

An extract from a page in the club's original minute book, dated Wednesday 29 April 1885, gives some indication of the good spirit that prevailed at that time:

> A hearty vote of thanks was proposed by Mr Harston to Mr Ripsher (with great cheering) for the kind way in which he had helped the Club financially and otherwise and also for the tea he had provided that evening. [Ripsher] said in reply that it was a great pleasure to have been able to help the Club in any way and he thought that the Club had [had], on the whole, a very successful season. They had, it was true, suffered more defeats than last season, but that, he was sure, was owing to the strong Clubs they had played, in fact they had sometimes been looked upon with contempt by Clubs who came down to play them owing to their age, but he was glad to say that the Tottenham Hotspur generally managed to give a good account of themselves.

It was not just the change of shirt colours that marked a new departure for the club in the 1885–86 season. Until then they had played only friendly matches but on 17 October 1885 they played in a cup competition for the first time. It was the first round of the London Association Cup and the first known club photograph was taken prior to the match with Ripsher and several of the founder members on it. A crowd of 400 at the Tottenham Marshes watched Hotspur achieve a memorable 5–2 victory over St Albans (a business team). Sadly, the joy of victory was to be short-lived. In the next round three weeks later Spurs were crushed 8–0 by the mighty Casuals, a team made up of the cream of public school old boys and university players. But results over the season as a whole were encouraging enough for the club to decide it would enter cup competitions again the following year.

The 1885–86 season was also marked by a change in the structure of the club. For the first time vice-presidents were elected, a total of five in all. One of them was John Howard Thompson, who provided another link between the club and All Hallows Church. Thompson was the churchwarden at All Hallows who, together with John Ripsher, had helped the Revd Alexander Wilson to found a branch of the Young Men's Church of England Society. He was the father of John Howard Thompson junior, one of the founder members of

Hotspur FC, and he had taken an active interest in the affairs of the club from the very beginning, always giving Ripsher his full support. Thompson was to remain involved with the club long after his son had ceased playing, and he played a key part in the move towards professionalism.

On Tuesday 20 April 1886 the club held the first of its annual dinners. It took place in an upstairs room of the Milford Tavern in Park Lane, Tottenham. Some 40 guests were present and John Ripsher, the president, was in the chair. In his speech, he pointed out with some pleasure 'that football was now running a close race with cricket as the national pastime of this country' due largely to 'the present scientific mode of playing the game'. In the course of the evening John Thompson senior gave well-deserved praise to Ripsher and told the audience of 'the high estimation in which Mr Ripsher was held by everyone in the Club'.

Another expulsion from headquarters

Early in the 1886–87 season the club was once again forced to leave its headquarters. For two years or so everything had gone well at Dorset Villas. The Hotspur boys had faithfully honoured their agreement with the Revd Wilson to attend church every Wednesday evening and they seem to have behaved themselves at the club's headquarters. But boys will be boys and once again it was their love of cards that was to prove their undoing. One Wednesday evening during a service at All Hallows, Wilson spotted a number of them doing the unthinkable: they were playing cards in one of the pews. The Victorian age was not one marked by soft indulgence of young people: discipline was strict and adults meant what they said. The boys could expect no leniency. Having forfeited the trust of the vicar by disrespecting the spirit of the agreement made with him, it was inevitable that they would be asked to leave Dorset Villas. And so, for the second time in its brief history, Tottenham Hotspur Football Club was made homeless.

But whatever their misdemeanours, there was one person who continued to stand by the boys in time of crisis – their faithful president and friend, John Ripsher. He immediately started the search for a new base and it was not long before he found rooms at the Red House Coffee Palace in Tottenham High Road, a building adjacent to

Spurs' present White Hart Lane ground. It was to prove a good choice of venue and it served as the club's headquarters for six years from 1886 until 1891. The boys liked it there, enjoying similar facilities as at Dorset Villas – including cards! The Red House was bought by the club in 1921. In 1934 a clock was fixed to the front and this was later surmounted by the figure of a cockerel. The building is now used by the club for administrative purposes and is known simply as 748 High Road.

During the 1886–87 season, dressing-room accommodation switched from Somerford Grove, off Park Lane, to the nearby Milford Tavern in Park Lane (venue of the annual dinner). This did not, however, shorten the distance the players had to walk to the Tottenham Marshes for home games. It was still about a mile from the dressing room to the pitch.

Despite upheavals off the pitch, Spurs made good progress on it. They entered two cup competitions, the London Association Cup and the East End Cup. Although they met with no success in the former, crashing out in the first round 6–0 to Upton Park, they reached the semi-final of the latter. It was played on the marshes on 16 April 1887. Spurs' opponents were the Caledonians, for whom Lord Kinnaird, football's first superstar, once played. The match ended in a 1–0 victory for the Caledonians. All other games played that season were friendlies and Spurs' record in them was more than respectable. Of the 20 games played, 14 were won and one was drawn; 59 goals were scored and 22 conceded.

The first match against Arsenal

The date 19 November 1887 is a significant one in the history of the club. It was the first meeting with the Royal Arsenal (now Arsenal), who were to become fierce local rivals but who at the time were barely one year old. The match was played at the Marshes. With only 15 minutes of the game remaining Spurs were leading 2–1 and seemed to have victory within their grasp, but failing light brought the game to a premature end and they were denied their first success against the club that was destined to become one of the greatest in the world. There would, however, be many more encounters between the two sides . . .

The first enclosed ground

The 1887–88 season was the last in which the club played its home matches on the Tottenham Marshes. It had been obvious for some time that the growing number of spectators who came to watch the team were getting out of control. There were frequent complaints by visiting teams about crowd behaviour. In an article in *The Football News* in 1900, P. J. Moss, who played for Spurs on the Marshes, paints a vivid picture of the last season there: 'In some of the games, with absolutely no gate money, it is no exaggeration to say that 4,000 spectators surrounded the field. They were not always considerate of the feelings of visiting teams and I well remember some East End Cup ties in which the visitors were pelted with mud, rotten turnips and other vegetable refuse.' There were also frequent complaints about foul language. This prompted one Spurs player to write to *The Herald* and say: 'It is utterly impossible to keep a public ground free from coarse personal remarks.'

But the situation could not be allowed to continue. Something had to be done. Four players – Bobby Buckle, Sam Casey, Frank Hatton and Jack Jull – took the initiative. They believed that if an enclosed private ground could be found, it would be possible to control the number of spectators at matches. Furthermore, an admission charge to the ground, as well as providing a useful source of revenue for the club, would discourage the more unruly element from turning up. When a pitch behind a garden nursery in Northumberland Park was discovered available for hire, the four players persuaded the committee to go ahead and hire it. Arrangements were made for dressing-room accommodation at the nearby Northumberland Arms tavern. And so, at the end of their sixth season, Spurs vacated the Marshes.

The first season at Northumberland Park (1888–89) saw the club become members of the Football Association. It was also marked by the success of Jack Jull who, at the age of 21, became the first Spurs player to receive representative honours. He was selected to play for Middlesex. Jull was one of the club's earliest players. He was a friend of many of the founder members because, like them, he had been a pupil of St John's Middle Class School, but during the club's first season he was away at boarding school and therefore did not register as a member. Such was his ability, however, that he was always included in the team when he was home on holiday or on a visit. He later became club captain.

One match early in 1888–89 is significant in showing how rapidly the club had developed in its short existence. Spurs had been started the same year – 1882 – that one of the most renowned teams in the country, the Old Etonians, had won the FA Cup. Yet, only six years later, on 13 October 1888, the two sides met at Northumberland Park in the first round of the London Senior Cup. Many of the Hotspur players were still only in their late teens. Predictably, the Old Etonians, with the famous Arthur Dunn in their side together with five other members of their 1882 FA Cup-winning team, had an easy 8–2 victory. Nevertheless, Spurs had rubbed shoulders with football's élite for the first time.

For the next three seasons the usual mix of friendlies and local cup competitions continued, but by 1892–93, Spurs' eleventh season, they had progressed sufficiently to embark upon league football. They joined the newly formed Southern Alliance. In this first season of league football, many of the faces from the early days had disappeared but the character of the club had changed very little. John Ripsher was still very much at the helm and he received able assistance from founder members Bobby Buckle and Sam Casey. Jack Jull, now aged 25 and in his tenth season with the club, was captain. Billy Harston, who was appointed vice-captain when Ripsher reconstituted the club in 1883, was also still in the side as were one or two other players from that time.

The legacy of John Ripsher

The following year, 1894, marked the end of an era. John Ripsher, the man described by Julian Holland in his 1956 history of Tottenham Hotspur as the club's 'midwife, nurse, father and teacher', decided to step down as president. After 11 years at the helm he felt the time had come to hand over to someone who could take the club forward to the next stage of its development. He duly resigned at the end of the 1893–94 season. His resignation was accepted with great regret, but it was no doubt some consolation to the club that at the start of the 1894–95 season he accepted the position of patron. Although this was merely an honorary position with no formal responsibilities, it meant that Ripsher's link with Spurs could continue and that he could observe developments from fairly close quarters.

And the developments moved along at a rapid pace. Within only seven years of Ripsher's retirement from the presidency, the club had turned professional (1895), become a limited company (1898), moved to White Hart Lane (1899), won the championship of the Southern League (1900), and won the FA Cup (1901) – still the only club outside the Football League ever to have done so. All this had happened within 18 years of Ripsher coming to the help of a few despondent schoolboys and welding them into a properly organized club. It shows the remarkable foundation he had laid for the club's growth and future success.

Ripsher had created such a strong spirit at the club that some of the boys who had been with him from the beginning remained actively involved in the direction of its affairs, even though he was no longer at the helm to guide them. At the 1896–97 AGM – the first as a professional club – John Thompson junior was the financial secretary, Bobby Buckle, Sam Casey and Fred Dexter were committee members, and Lindsay Casey and Stuart Leaman were the auditors. When the club became a limited company in 1898 under the name of The Tottenham Hotspur Football and Athletic Company Limited, Bobby Buckle and John Thompson junior were elected to the board of directors. Evidence of the good spirit that had always prevailed at the club appears in the famous history of the game, *Association Football & The Men Who Made It* (published in 1906), where it is recorded that 'the good-fellowship which characterized the early stages of the club's history still exists, despite change of circumstances and rise to fame. I have no hesitation in saying that there is no club in the country in which there is better feeling between the players and the directors . . . than at Tottenham.'

But Ripsher created more than a good spirit at the club. Under his leadership, Spurs also established a reputation for fair play and good sportsmanship that made them the most popular club in England. This reputation lasted well into the twentieth century. In 1948, Fred Ward, author of a history of the club, was asked by the editor of a northern sports newspaper: 'Why is it that when we up north speak of the Hotspur we always use language that is respectful?' The answer Ward gave is revealing:

In the first place, most of the club's controllers in the past have played the game and, consequently, know that unfair tactics get a club nowhere that is creditable or advantageous. They do not wait for one of their players to be sent off the field by a referee . . . At Tottenham they are their own disciplinarians. If one of their men goes beyond the pale of sportsmanship, or even shows a tendency to do so, he is called before the Board at the first opportunity and told that there is no place for him in the team if he adopts foul play as a means of beating opponents.

Ward attributes the tradition of good sportsmanship at the club to John Ripsher:

> Let us pause awhile here and think of what that excellent Mr Ripsher did. He started a tradition in the Hotspur club which has been maintained up to the present time, for, in my opinion, Tottenham Hotspur Football Club . . . have done much to perpetuate the best possible spirit in the playing of professional soccer.

Ripsher had well and truly left his mark on the club, but what became of the great man himself? He was a patron for a few years after he had retired from the presidency, but the only mention we have of him in his later years appears in the 1908 history of the club: 'It came as a great shock to us to learn that he is now living at Dover in humble circumstances and is totally blind.' Ripsher, who never married, left Tottenham for Dover to join his sister Jane who lived there with her husband, William Baker. William was the proprietor of the Diamond Hotel in Dover and in 1901 Ripsher was living there with Jane, William, their daughter, son and a domestic servant and barmaid. Ripsher was working as a clerk in a steam laundry at the time but later moved to a similar position in an iron foundry.

By 1906 Ripsher had developed severe health problems and the final two years of his life must have been extremely distressing. It seems that the decline in his health had been accompanied by a decline in his (and possibly also William and Jane's) material circumstances because, on 14 January 1906, he was admitted to the workhouse in Union Road, Dover, an institution where medical care was provided for the poor and the destitute of the town. He spent two periods there in 1906 – from 14 January to 14 July and from 23 August to 24 September. He was admitted again on 13 March 1907 but this time he was never to leave. He died on 24 September, aged 67, of heart problems. Four days later, on 28 September, he was buried at St Mary's Cemetery in Old Charlton Road, Dover, in an unmarked pauper's grave.

It is ironic that the man, in the words of the 1908 club history, who had 'spent a small fortune' and had given his time 'wet or fine, year in and year out, every night until 10 o'clock' to establish a club that was destined to become one of the richest in England, should die in an institution for paupers. Poor he may have been at the end of his days, but Tottenham Hotspur Football Club will forever be in the debt of John Ripsher, the Bible class teacher from All Hallows Church.

Afterword

GEOFF THOMPSON
CHAIRMAN OF THE FOOTBALL ASSOCIATION

———•◆•———

The Christian pioneers of football of yesteryear reached out to their communities and enriched them considerably. But pioneering outreach work in football continues today. Geoff Thompson, Chairman of The Football Association and a committed Christian, set up an initiative in 2000 – the International Development Programme (IDP) – which he sees as a natural extension of the work begun by people featured in this book. Thompson firmly believes in building relationships with the football family around the world by sharing The FA's expertise and resources, particularly with less privileged nations. He has energetically pursued this goal through the IDP and he has led the expansion of the programme around the world. He has specially written the following piece for inclusion in this book. In it he draws a parallel between the pioneers of yesterday and the work of The FA abroad today:

I have been inspired by the dedication and example of many people featured in this book, especially by their concern for the welfare of the underprivileged in their communities. I share both their faith in Christ and their desire to reach out to others less fortunate than themselves.

The international work of The FA is special to me because it is a unique way of extending the hand of friendship to all corners of the world and of improving the lives of others through football.

For the main part, our programmes focus on training coaches, referees and football administrators; on education, improving skills and raising the standards of football. We also provide much needed equipment such as football kit and balls, often in response to natural disasters which devastate communities. Following the tsunami in 2004, we responded to FIFA's appeal for equipment for the Indonesian island of Aceh, our donation bringing some joy to a community which had experienced so much suffering and lost so much.

Increasingly, we are exploring the power of football as a vehicle for social development. Football can be an incredibly binding force and as such, a great champion of peace. We saw this for ourselves in Afghanistan when, at the end of 23 years of war, we were invited to stage a football match in the stricken Olympic Stadium in Kabul. Over 25,000 watched this game, which featured an Afghan team and one made up of the international security forces, united in their love of football and their celebration of peace.

In Africa, we recognize that the power of football extends far beyond the development of the game itself. We have three partner countries – Botswana, Lesotho and Malawi – all of which are being ravaged by the HIV virus. Life expectancy is under 40 in each of these countries; the effects of the disease are truly shocking.

With the assistance of specialist partners, we have worked at integrating HIV awareness messages into our footballing training courses. Three of our current England senior team players – Rio Ferdinand, Gary Neville and David James – joined us in Malawi. In a country where only some 20 per cent of the population has access to a television, such is the passion for football that these players were nevertheless rapturously received. They were instantly able to engage with young people, helping to deliver the message 'My goal is life . . . prevent HIV' with amazing effect. Their lives, too, have been changed by their experience.

Many of the Christians who created great football clubs also understood that football had an opportunity to change lives, inspire and motivate. They, too, were active in their immediate localities and parishes, reaching out to the underprivileged and the helpless on their doorstep. Today our doorstep is the entire world but the spirit that moves us is the same spirit that moved those early pioneers.

As we work around the world, developing our beloved game, we are indeed touching communities far and wide, irrespective of whether they speak our language, whether the colour of their skin is different to ours, whether they are older or younger, whether they are boys or girls. What really matters is that we share an interest in joining together, kicking a ball together, sharing experiences together and learning together.

It is indeed a great privilege for me, and for The FA, to be involved in such work; to see the joy that football can bring, and particularly to witness how it can enhance the lives of those less privileged than ourselves. We are truly blessed.

Geoff Thompson's work on behalf of poorer nations has been warmly applauded abroad and many expressions of appreciation have been made to him. He remembers one occasion in particular. At a conference at the headquarters of CONMEBOL (the South American Football Confederation) in Asunción, Paraguay, in September 2003, he gave his opening speech and then, to his complete surprise, the Order of Merit of South American Football was conferred upon him. Nicolas Leoz, the president of CONMEBOL, wrote to him afterwards saying: 'With your visit, you have sealed a friendship that brings us close together, both in terms of personal affection and professional work. The doors to the Home of South American football will always be open to you. My best wishes for continued success as Head of football of the nation that created the sport that has given people around the world so many satisfactions.'

Geoff Thompson is admirably upholding the tradition of the pioneers to whom this book pays tribute.

Index

Twenty Years in Soho (Cardwell) 76, 87
Tyas, C. J. 23, 24
Tyrell, William 148

United Church, Liverpool 59

Varley, A. 124
Vulcan Football Club 109

Wade, Alfred Riley 56, 60, 69, 71
Wade, Joseph 55–7
Walker, Revd Hyde Edwardes 75
Wall, Edward 146–7
Walsall Town Football Club 11
Ward, Fred 157
Warmley Football Club 127
Wasps Rugby Club 84
Watson, A. 136
Watts, Alan 41
Wednesbury Old Athletic 6, 38
Weiss, W. 5
Weller, Fred 108, 109, 112, 116–17
West Bromwich Albion Football Club 11, 28, 115
West Gorton *see* Manchester; Manchester City Football Club
West London Association Cup 84
West London League 85, 113–14
West London Observer Challenge Cup 84

Whateley, H. 5
White, A. 60
Wilberforce, Canon Basil 120–2, 123, 126, 129
Williams, Revd William 4
Williams, W. (Everton) 60
Wilson, Revd Alexander 150, 151, 152, 153
Wiltshire Senior Cup 138
Wodehouse, George (*fils*) 116
Wodehouse, George (*père*) 110, 116
Wolverhampton Wanderers Football Club 11
Womack, Frank 42
Woolford, W. 136
Woolwich Arsenal Football Club 115
Wright, Arthur 34
Wright, Ellen 44–5
Wright, Joseph Farrall (*fils*) 51–2
Wright, Revd Joseph (*père*) 43–5, 51; football club and 47–9, 49–50; partnership with Ogden 46–7

Young, Revd Charles 110–11, 117
Young Men's Association (YMA) 122, 125–7
Young Men's Christian Association (YMCA) 135, 148, 149–51
Young Men's Church of England Society 152
Yoxall, H. S. 2–3